PAINLESS
Spelling

Second Edition

Mary Elizabeth, M.Ed.

illustrated by Hank Morehouse

BARRON'S

All inquiries should be addressed to:
Barron's Educational Series, Inc.
250 Wireless Boulevard
Hauppauge, New York 11788
http://www.barronseduc.com

Library of Congress Catalog Card No.: 2006042736

ISBN-13: 978-0-7641-3435-7
ISBN-10: 0-7641-3435-3

Library of Congress Cataloging-in-Publication Data

Mary Elizabeth (Mary Elizabeth Podhaizer)
  Painless spelling, second edition / Mary Elizabeth.—2nd ed.
    p.   cm.
  Includes index.
  ISBN-13: 978-0-7641-3435-7
  ISBN-10: 0-7641-3435-3
  1. English language—Orthography and spelling—Study and teaching (Elementary)—Juvenile literature.   2. English language—Orthography and spelling—Study and teaching (Middle school)—Juvenile literature.   I. Title.
  LB1574.P63   2006
  372.63'2—dc22   2006042736

PRINTED IN CANADA
9 8 7 6 5 4

This book is for Fr. Paa Kwesi Maison
and everyone—
born in the United States or elsewhere—
who tries to make sense of
English spelling.

Acknowledgments

Thank you to the authors of *Words Their Way: Word Study for Phonics, Vocabulary, and Spelling Instruction,* whose intelligent and insightful developmental approach to spelling provided the categories around which I organized this book.

CONTENTS

INTRODUCTION

Which is correct: *cosily* or *cozily? theater* or *theatre? traveler* or *traveller?* The answer may surprise you: they are ALL correct. And that's the first problem with spelling in English—sometimes there's more than one correct way to write a word. But that's only the beginning. Teeming with words borrowed from other languages, English can seem like an impossible language to spell correctly. Not to worry. This book will take you on a tour of U.S. English and help you nail down the basics that will make spelling most English words less of a challenge.

Sure, you'll still run across words that are exceptions to the rules you learn because any word in a U.S. English dictionary, no matter what its origin, is considered English, and as a result, we have to work with spelling rules from many different languages of origin. For example, if you want to spell *qiviut*, the Inuit word for the undercoat of the musk ox, you have to ignore the general rule that *q* is always followed by *u*. But for the most part, the

guidelines in this book will help you steer cleanly through the inconsistencies in the strange and wonderful language we call English.

These days, some folks are saying that spelling is not very important. They argue that since most people do most of their writing on a computer, and using the spell checker is a cinch, we don't need to focus on spelling. Don't get taken in by this reasoning! If you type *through* instead of *threw*, or *their* instead of *there*, or *even* instead of *event*, your spell checker can't tell that you made a mistake—all six are perfectly good and correctly spelled English words. One study found that as many as 40 percent of spelling errors are real-word errors in which one word is mistakenly typed for another.

In addition, if you type *eggzasparated* instead of *exasperated*, your spell checker may not have a clue about what word you MEANT to type (mine didn't!). And if you're walking by the

Eggzasparated!?

sporting goods store and see that they're holding interviews today, and you have to fill out a job application for them, you won't get a chance to spell-check your writing. The people who are doing the hiring will judge you on your spelling, among other things. You'll want to be prepared with a good, broad knowledge of how to spell English words.

The fact is, no matter how many gadgets and gizmos you have to help you, you still need to know fundamental spelling rules in order to communicate with people. And that's the whole point! We don't learn spelling rules for the sake of learning the rules. The goal is to express ourselves in a way that others can understand. THAT'S the reason to learn more about spelling.

We begin by talking about visual and sound patterns in English. Then we go on a tour of the patterns that will help you learn or review the combinations you see and hear every day. Exercises will help you understand the relationships between spoken and written language and become more aware of the structure of written words and the relationships between and among words. They will also help you become more familiar with the characteristic patterns of English spelling. You can jot down your answers to the exercises on loose-leaf paper or in a notebook. By the time we're finished, you'll be able to spend more time thinking about what you're communicating instead of how to spell it correctly. And that's where it's at!

(The dictionary we'll be using as our point of reference, unless otherwise noted, is *The American Heritage Dictionary of the English Language*.)

THE HISTORY OF ENGLISH

Do you know what a mongrel is? Sometimes we use the word *mongrel* to refer to a dog with a mixed background. So you can think of it as meaning "a mixture." The English language is a mixture in this sense.

The English language came into being around AD 450. Three tribes from Northern Europe—the Angles, the Saxons, and the Jutes—invaded the British Isles. The main island came to be known as jolly old "Angle"land (England), and the language that came into being became known as Anglo-Saxon or **Old English**. Every one of the top 100 most frequently used words in English today comes from Old English.

BRAIN TICKLERS
Set # 1

Hey, that was some generalization about the top 100 words in English! What are the most frequently used words in English, anyway? And do they really come from Old English? To check it out yourself, follow these directions.

1. Choose one page of text in a book. Use any book that is primarily complete sentences (not a dictionary) and is written in English.

2. Count how many times each word appears and keep tabs. You might want to use tally marks. This won't exactly give you the top 100 most frequently used words in English, but it will give you an idea of some words that are used pretty often.

3. Look up the most frequently used words in a dictionary. Check out the etymological information in the entry (the part that tells what language the word comes from).

4. Compare your findings with someone else, if possible. What are the similarities? The differences?

(Answers are on page xv.)

Getting back to the history of English. . . . In about AD 600, the language began to change because St. Augustine came to Britain, bringing Christianity and a lot of Latin words. People started learning to write English, and so English spelling was invented.

But then more invasions brought more new words into English. The Viking invasions began in the late 700s, bringing Danish words. Then, in 1066, came William the Conqueror and the Normans, bringing French words. After a couple of hundred years, the differences that resulted from the addition of French had become so great that the change in the language has a name. We call the mixture of Old English with French that was spoken starting in the early 1200s **Middle English**. Just to let you know how that influence has lasted, about 40 percent of all English words used today have French origins.

The rediscovery of Greek and Latin classics in the period of the Renaissance (1300s to 1600s) and the introduction of the printing press in the 1400s brought many new words to England. All these new additions to the language kept things very unsettled until the mid-1700s, when English spelling began to become standardized as the result of the publication of a definitive dictionary by Samuel Johnson—and this is when **Modern English** began.

But those aren't all the sources for English!! Not by a long shot. Here's a sampling of fairly common English words and their sources:

Word	Language of Origin	Word	Language of Origin
algebra	Arabic	matzo	Yiddish
bolero	Spanish	pizza	Italian
boomerang	Dhaurk (Australian Aborigine language)	skunk	Algonquian
chipmunk	Ojibwa	tepee	Dakota
futon	Japanese	wok	Chinese
ketchup or catsup	Malay	yak	Tibetan

BRAIN TICKLERS
Set # 2

1. Look at this list of ten common English words that have come into English from another language. Use a dictionary to look up each word's etymology. The dictionary will begin with the language from which the word came most recently and work back to the language of ultimate origin. Briefly tell in what language the word began and how it traveled into English.

| artichoke | boss | cooky or cookie | jungle | oboe |
| raccoon | robot | sponge | tea | teak |

2. Choose a word that you think may have come into English from another language. Check in a dictionary to see if you are right. Keep checking until you find one. Write down the word and the language it originally started in.

(Answers are on page xv.)

Understanding a little about the sources of English will help you understand why there are several different patterns of spelling in modern English. Each language of origin has its own rules for representing sounds with letters. In addition, the pronunciation of English has changed over time. So sounds are not represented by letters in English in a one-to-one correspondence. (We'll talk more about this beginning in Chapter 2.) This book will help you spell English words by calling your attention to the patterns of spelling and by helping you understand what you can expect from English words.

BRAIN TICKLERS—
THE ANSWERS

Set # 1, page xi

Answers will vary depending on the material you have chosen. The most frequently used word in this entire introduction (pages vii–xiv; 1,385 words) is (can you guess?) *the*. It appears 90 times. And guess what! It's from Old English. Here are some other frequently used words in this chapter—all from Old English.

of 46 times   **you** 33 times
English 46 times   **and** 30 times
to 39 times   **word** 23 times
in 35 times   **that** 21 times
a 34 times

Set # 2, page xiv

Answers may vary depending on the dictionary used.
1. **artichoke**   Arabic to Old Spanish to Italian to English
   boss   Germanic to Middle Dutch to Dutch to English
   cooky or cookie   Middle Dutch to Dutch to English
   jungle   Sanskrit to Hindi and Marathi to English
   oboe   French to Italian to English
   raccoon   Algonquin to English
   robot   Czech to English
   sponge   Greek to Latin to Old English to Middle English
   tea   Ancient Chinese to Amoy to Malay to Dutch to English
   teak   Malayalam to Portuguese to English

2. Answers will vary. Possible responses:
   café Turkish   **pharaoh** Egyptian
   curry Tamil   **sierra** Latin
   galore Irish Gaelic   **soy** Mandarin Chinese
   galoshes Old French   **squirrel** Greek
   knack Middle Dutch   **taco** Spanish
   mesa Latin   **tortilla** Late Latin
   omelet Latin

Part One

INTRODUCTION TO LETTER PATTERNS

CHAPTER ONE

Letter Patterns

SPELLING IN ENGLISH

This section will get you warmed up for the kind of work you'll be doing in the rest of the book. It is based on the idea that there is a relationship between what you see when you look at a word written down, and what you hear when a word is spoken aloud. Because this relationship is not always clear, sometimes you have to analyze a word to understand it.

What IS correct spelling?

People are fond of pointing out that even Shakespeare, that great master of the written word, was known to spell his own last name in different ways at different times. In fact, the goal of having a single correct spelling for a word is a fairly new idea. For years and years, nobody thought that spelling the same word in different ways was such a problem. Spelling of English started to become regular in the 1600s to 1700s.

And would you believe that after several hundred years of trying to regularize our spelling, we still haven't managed? In the 1970s—not that long ago in the history of English—Lee C. Deighton compared four of the major American English dictionaries and found considerable disagreement about the "right" way to spell several thousand common English words. Not only do the dictionaries all offer multiple correct spellings, but they often disagree with each other about how to spell the words.

Here are some examples. How do you spell the word we usually say when we part company? Well, according to Deighton's study, it could be *good-by, goodby, good-bye,* or *goodbye.* If you're scared, you might be *chickenhearted,* or you might be *chicken-hearted.* That healthy stuff you ate for lunch might be *yogurt, yoghurt,* or *yoghourt.* And a song that is traditionally sung to a newly married couple takes the cake! It can be spelled *shivaree, charivaree, chivaree, chivari,* or *charivari.* Is that confusing, or what?

BRAIN TICKLERS
Set # 3

1. Here are some words that have more than one correct spelling in English. Using a dictionary at home, in the library or at school, or on the Internet, find at least one alternate spelling for each word. Record your findings. Hint: The spellings below are from the *American Heritage Dictionary,* so you might want to try using a different one.

clear-headed	per cent	teen-age
corn flakes	retrorocket	

2. How many different spellings can you find for the word *boogieman*? Write down the names of the dictionaries or on-line sources you used and the spellings you found.

(Answers are on page 30.)

Nobody is ever finished learning to spell

It's important to realize that learning to spell is a process that isn't complete for anyone. As you've seen, even the experts can't agree on how to spell a large number of words correctly. In addition, new words are constantly being added to English as people create new concepts and invent equipment with new names and as slang terms and phrases arise. Besides that, as each of us learns new subject areas and skills, we need a new vocabulary so we can talk about our experience.

It's true that some people have an easier time spelling than others. But spelling is something that everyone has to pay attention to. So now let's look at the way we learn to spell.

We start with sound

Think about how people learn language. Maybe you have a younger brother or sister, or maybe a baby lives next door to you. Do they start off learning English by trying to write words? Of course not! They listen to people speak English, and they begin by learning that the sounds they hear can be understood as words, each of which MEANS something. To them, *dog* is a group of sounds that refers to a furry, four-legged beast that licks their faces.

And that's the key to thinking about words—words are sounds written down. After you figure this out—after you understand that written words are a code for the sounds of words spoken aloud—you can learn to read and write. And eventually you get to the point at which you realize that if you want to be understood easily, you have to write n-o, and not n-o-a or n-o-e.

But this is where English can get confusing, because if you want to write the word *boat*, you spell the same sound that you hear in *no* but with the letters *o-a;* and if you want to write the word *doe*, you spell it *o-e*. The job of this book is to help you figure out the different ways to spell the sounds you hear by giving you rules and strategies. Then you can understand and remember the different patterns for recording the sounds of English. And the most important tool for making sound patterns in writing is, of course, the alphabet.

The alphabet

Okay. We've got the English alphabet with 26 letters. And each letter, by itself, can represent one or more sounds. (For example, you probably know by now that the vowels can have a long or short pronunciation and that the letter *c* can be pronounced like the letter *k* or like the letter *s*, depending on the context.)

But when you put letters together, you can record some sounds that you can't record with a single letter, AND you can duplicate some sounds that you could already make with one letter. (For example, the letters *ow* spell a sound that you can't spell with one letter, but *ph* can indicate the same sound as *f* does by itself.)

And when you put some letters next to others, the sound changes. (For example, an *r* following a vowel can change the pronunciation of the vowel.)

This sounds really complicated. And some people get really upset about it. The British playwright George Bernard Shaw scoffed that you could just as well spell *fish* as *ghoti* if you used *gh* from *rough*, *o* from *women*, and *ti* from *nation*. The problem of spelling was so important to Shaw, that when he died, he left A LOT of his money for the purpose of trying to reform English spelling so it would have one, and only one, symbol for each sound. But it didn't happen.

BRAIN TICKLERS
Set # 4

Make up a new spelling of a word the same way George Bernard Shaw did. Share it with a classmate or friend, and see if he or she can figure out what word you spelled.

(Answers are on page 31.)

The patterns

As we've already pointed out, some sounds can be spelled in more than one way. This makes English more complicated than, say, Spanish, in which each letter has just one pronunciation (on the whole). But there IS a limit. Some people would rather not know about the complications. But my approach to difficulties is to examine them to see what you've got: Once you know where you stand, you can plunge in and try to come to terms with whatever it is. So that's what I'm going to try to help you do.

BRAIN TICKLERS
Set # 5

Read each word aloud. Listen to the sound represented by the bold letter(s). Try to think of other words in which the same sound is spelled in a different way. Write down all the words you think of—the more the better. DON'T LOOK AHEAD AT THE CHART ON PAGE 16 UNLESS YOU'RE REALLY, REALLY STUCK.

1. m**a**d
2. b**i**t
3. m**e**
4. n**o**
5. le**af**
6. **sh**oe
7. **t**iger

(Answers are on page 31.)

One word: multiple spellings

Sometimes there is more than one correct way to spell or pronounce a word. Why? Well, there are a few reasons.

1. The spelling of some words has changed over time. For example, *town* used to be spelled with an *e* on the end—*towne*.

2. U.S. and British spelling have become differentiated. The British commonly:
   use a double *l* where we use a single *l* (*traveller* vs. *traveler*),
   use *ou* in cases where we use just an *o* (*colour* vs. *color*),
   use an *re* ending where we use an *er* ending (*metre* vs. *meter*),
   use a *ce* ending where we use an *se* ending (*defence* vs. *defense*),
   and keep an *e* between syllables where we drop it (*judgement* vs. *judgment*).

3. There are some spellings that have become acceptable in advertising and brand names:
doughnut can become *donut*
light can become *lite*
night can become *nite*
school can become *skool*

4. Some foreign words have entered our language through multiple avenues and so continue to have multiple spellings. Remember *shivaree* (page 6)? It comes to us through French.

   If a word has multiple pronunciations or spellings that are acceptable, the dictionary will have multiple entries for it. The first entry is preferred, but all of the entries are correct and accurate English.

Some helpful words

We will have an easier time talking and thinking about spelling if we have some vocabulary to name some special spelling concepts and some symbols to show special usage.

blend A consonant blend has two distinct sounds that follow one after the other. Some blends are written with two consonant letters (for example, *st*) and some have three letters (for example, *str*). All blends include either an *l* (as in *bl*), an *m* (as in *mp*), an *n* (as in *sn*), an *r* (as in *gr*), an *s* (as in *sp*), or a *w* (as in *tw*). Some blends have more than one of these letters.

consonant/vowel Consonants and vowels are sounds, not letters. There are consonant letters (*k, l, m, n, x*) and vowel letters (*a, e, i, o, u*, and *y*). Sometimes the letters we call consonant letters are used as auxiliary letters in spelling a vowel. For example,

> *gh* helps spell the long *i* sound in the word *sigh*

> *w* helps spell the vowel sound /ow/ in the word *cow*

Some consonant sounds are spelled using "vowel" letters.

> *u* spells the /w/ sound in the word *quick*

> *y* can represent either a vowel sound, as in *happy*, or a consonant sound, as in *yes*

digraph Literally, a digraph is a string of two letters, which may be either vowel letters or consonant letters (*di-* means "two" and *graph* means "letter"). One specialized meaning is "a group of two or three consonant letters that represent a new sound, different from the sounds represented by any of the individual consonant letters by itself."

Examples of consonant letter digraphs are
shoe /sh/
church /ch/
thirst /th/ and
than /*th*/

diphthong A diphthong is a vowel sound that changes during its production. If you say VERY slowly the words *brown, bite,* and *boy,* you will probably hear the vowel sound change at the same time as you feel your mouth move. Each of those words has a vowel diphthong.

phoneme A phoneme is any single sound. A particular phoneme may have one or more spellings.

// Slash marks are used to show sounds. The slash marks let you know that what follows is not letters or words:

a is a word, the English indefinite article; we use italics to show words and letters.

/ă/ is the vowel sound in the first syllable of the word *Batman.*

The dictionary used for sounds, symbols, meaning, and pronunciation in this book is *The American Heritage Dictionary of the English Language.* The symbols used in this book for the sounds of words are the symbols used in the first entry of a word in *The American Heritage Dictionary.*

pronunciation Although some pronunciations are simply "wrong," there is often more than one correct way to say a word. This is because pronunciation of English varies. A teacher may be able to help you identify which differences are because of dialect (the version of English you speak) and which might be caused by mispronunciation.

How do you spell . . . ?

The charts on the following pages will show you the range of possibilities for spelling some of the main sounds of English. You'll see some patterns that you found when you did Brain Ticklers Set # 5, and maybe you'll also see some you didn't think of. You DON'T have to memorize them. You might want to put a sticky note on the first page so you can find it again.

- Since people pronounce words differently, some of the words in the chart may appear to you to be in the wrong place. (An * will call your attention to some of these words.) Don't worry about it now.

- _ stands for a consonant letter. So, for example, *a_e* could represent *ate, ace, age,* or *ape*.

- A letter combination can appear anywhere in a word, or be an entire word in itself.

  agent (beginning)   dr**ape**r (middle)
  N**ate** (end)   **ace** (whole word)

- **Common** indicates the most frequently occurring spellings of the sound. **Less Common** indicates spellings that are less frequently seen. **Oddball** refers to spellings that are very rare and may even be unique. Some have come into English from another language and may retain characteristic spelling patterns from their language of origin. Consult this column only if it is useful to you.

- How do we understand the role of silent letters here? It might seem to make sense to leave them out: after all, a silent letter doesn't spell any sound. But this approach does not help us remember spelling patterns. For this reason, silent letters are included. If you prefer (or are directed to take) a different approach, feel free to ignore or cross out these examples.

- All words in the chart represent the first pronunciation in the *American Heritage Dictionary* unless there is a note saying *2ⁿᵈ*, which indicates that the second pronunciation is meant.

- Different dialects of English treat the sounds represented by *American Heritage* as ä, ô, and ŏ very differently. In another major dictionary, ô and ŏ are treated as the same sound. In a third, ä and ŏ are treated as the same. To avoid confusion, these sounds are not included in the chart.

SOUND Short Vowel Sounds	SPELLINGS		
	Common	Less Common	Oddball
short a /ă/	**a** as in *bat*	**a_ _e** as in *trance* **al** as in *half* **au** as in *laugh* **i** as in *meringue*	**a_e** as in *comrade* **ai** as in *plaid*
short e /ĕ/	**e** as in *bet* **ea** as in *bread*	**a** as in *any* **ai** as in *said* **ei** as in *leisure** **eo** as in *leopard* **u** as in *bury* **ue** as in *guess*	**ie** as in *friend* **ay** as in *says* **é** as in *créme* **oe** as in *roentgen*
short i /ĭ/	**e** as in *English* **i** as in *bit* **a_e** as in *advantage*	**ia** as in *carriage* **u** as in *busy* **y** as in *abyss*	**i_ _e** as in *grippe* **ie_e** as in *sieve* **o** as in *women* **ui** as in *build* **ee** as in *been*
short u /ŭ/ in an accented syllable	**o** as in *oven* **u** as in *but*	**oo** as in *flood* **ou** as in *trouble*	**e** as in *them*—2nd **o_e** as in *come* **oe** as in *doesn't* **au_e** as in *because* _2nd
schwa /ə/ in an unaccented syllable	**a** as in *balloon* **e** as in *concentration* **o** as in *prison* **u** as in *circus*	**ai** as in *captain* **eo** as in *dungeon* **i** as in *pencil* **ia** as in *special* **iou** as in *anxious* **ou** as in *generous*	**é** as in *protégé* (1st é) **eu** as in *chauffeur*
/o͞o/	**o** as in *woman* **u** as in *bull*	**ou** as in *could* **oo** as in *wood*	**oui** as in *bouillon* _2nd

16

SOUND Long Vowel Sounds	SPELLINGS		
	Common	Less Common	Oddball
long a /ā/	a as in *favor* a_e as in *male* a_ _e as in *paste* ai as in *mail* ai_e as in *praise* ay as in *may*	ae as in *Gaelic* é as in *soufflé* ée as in *née* e_e as in *crepe* ea as in *great* ee as in *matinee* ei as in *veil* eig as in *deign* eigh as in *neighbor* et as in *bouquet* ey as in *prey*	aig as in *arraign* aigh as in *straight* ao as in *gaol* au_e as in *gauge* aye as in *aye* (always) e as in *rodeo*–2nd eh as in *eh* oeh as in *foehn*–2nd (u)ay as in *quay*–2nd
long e /ē/	e as in *me* e_e as in *gene* ea as in *peal* ee as in *peek* y as in *happy*	ae as in *archaeology* ay as in *quay* ea_e as in *peace* ei_e as in *receive* ie as in *thief* ie_e as in *believe* ey as in *key* i as in *curious* i_e as in *machine* is as in *chassis* oe as in *phoenix* uy as in *soliloquy*	a as in *bologna* eo as in *people* (u)ay as in *quay*
long i /ī/	i as in *mild* i_e as in *mile* ie as in *lie* igh as in *might* y as in *my*	ai as in *Thailand* ay as in *papaya* ei as in *stein* eigh as in *height* eye as in *eye* ia as in *vial*–2nd ig as in *sign* is as in *island* uy as in *buy* ye as in *bye* y_e as in *rhyme*	ai_ _e as in *faille* ais as in *aisle* aye as in *aye* (yea) oy as in *coyote* ui_e as in *guide* uye as in *guyed*
long o /ō/	o as in *no* o_e as in *mole* oa as in *moat* oe as in *doe* ow as in *mow*	au as in *chauvinist* eau as in *plateau* oh as in *oh* ol as in *folk* ou as in *soul* ough as in *though* owe as in *owe*	aoh as in *pharaoh* aux as in *faux* eo as in *yeoman* eou as in *Seoul* ew as in *sew* ho as in *mho* ô_e as in *côte* oo as in *brooch* ot as in *tarot*
long u /o͞o/	ew as in *stew* o as in *to* oo as in *soon* o_e as in *whose* u as in *Ruth* u_e as in *June*	eu as in *sleuth* oe as in *canoe* ou as in *you* ue as in *blue* ui as in *suit*	ieu as in *adieu*–2nd ough as in *through* oup as in *coup* ou_e as in *coupe* ou_ _e as in *mousse* ougha as in *brougham* wo as in *two*
long u with y in front /yo͞o/	ew as in *ewe* u as in *human* u_e as in *mule*	eu as in *feud* iew as in *view* ue as in *barbecue* you as in *youth*	eau as in *beauty* ieu as in *adieu* u_ _e as in *butte* ueue as in *queue*

SOUND Vowel Sounds	SPELLINGS		
	Common	Less Common	Oddball
/oi/	**oi** as in *boil* **oy** as in *boy*		**oig** as in *coign* **uoi** as in *quoin* **uoy** as in *buoy*
/ou/	**ou** as in *cloud* **ow** as in *frown*	**hou** as in *hour* **ough** as in *bough*	**ao** as in *Tao* **aue** as in *sauerbraten* **iao** as in *ciao*
/âr/	**air** as in *lair* **ar** as in *parent* **are** as in *snare* **ear** as in *pear*	**aer** as in *aerobic* **aire** as in *millionaire* **er** as in *scherzo* **eyr** as in *eyrie*	**ayer** as in *prayer* (not the person, who's a /prã´ ər/) **e'er** as in *e'er* **ere** as in *ere* **eyre** as in *eyre* **heir** as in *heir* **iere** as in *premiere–2nd* **uar** as in *guarantee*
/îr/	**ear** as in *dear* **eer** as in *deer* **er** as in *zero* **ere** as in *here*	**eir** as in *weird* **ier** as in *tier*	**aer** as in *aerie–2nd* **eor** as in *theory* **eyr** as in *eyrie–2nd* **iere** as in *premiere* **ière** as in *première* **yr** as in *Tyr*
/ôr/	**ar** as in *quarrel* **or** as in *condor* **ore** as in *galore*	**aur** as in *centaur* **oar** as in *roar* **oor** as in *door* **our** as in *four*	**awr** as in *Lawrence* **oe** as in *Boer–2nd* **or** as in *torr*
/ûr/	**er** as in *kernel* **eur** as in *entrepreneur* **ir** as in *bird* **ur** as in *burn*	**ear** as in *learn* **ere** as in *were* **irr** as in *whirr* **or** as in *work* **our** as in *courtesy* **urr** as in *burr* **yr** as in *myrtle*	**olo** as in *colonel* **yrrh** as in *myrrh*

SOUND Vowel Sounds	SPELLINGS		
	Common	Less Common	Oddball
/ch/	**ch** as in *chimp* **tch** as in *watch*	**c(e)** as in *cello* **t(e)** as in *righteous* **t(i)** as in *question* **t(ure)** as in *creature*	**cz** as in *Czech*
/f/	**f** as in *leaf* **ph** as in *photo*	**ff** as in *difficult* **ft** as in *often* **gh** as in *tough* **lf** as in *calf*	
/g/	**g** as in *girl* **gg** as in *egg*	**gh** as in *ghost* **gue** as in *dialogue* **x** as in *exam*	
/h/	**h** as in *human*	**g** as in *Gila monster* **j** as in *junta* **wh** as in *who*	
/j/	**dg(e)** as in *judge* **g(e)** as in *gentle* **j** as in *jump*	**dg(i)** as in *lodging* **g(i)** as in *giraffe* **d(u)** as in *graduate*	**d(i)** as in *soldier* **dj(e)** as in *adjective* **g(a)** as in *gaol* **gg(e)** as in *exaggerate*
/k/	**c** as in *camel* **ck** as in *back* **k** as in *kangaroo* **q(u)** as in *conquer*	**cc** as in *accurate* **ch** as in *ache* **cq(u)** as in *lacquer* **kh** as in *khaki* **lk** as in *walk* **que** as in *oblique*	**cch** as in *saccharine* **kk** as in *trekked* **q** as in *FAQ* **q(i)** as in *Iraqi* **x** as in *exceed*
/l/	**l** as in *late* **ll** as in *troll*	**sl** as in *isle*	**lh** as in *lhasa apso* **ln** as in *kiln–2nd*

LETTER PATTERNS

SOUND Consonant Sounds	SPELLINGS		
	Common	Less Common	Oddball
/m/	**m** as in *mom* **mm** as in *mommy*	**gm** as in *diaphragm* **lm** as in *calm* **mb** as in *lamb* **mn** as in *limn*	**chm** as in *drachm*
/n/	**n** as in *pin* **nn** as in *inn*	**gn** as in *gnat* **kn** as in *knee* **mn** as in *mnemonic* **nd** as in *handsome* **pn** as in *pneumonia*	**dn** as in *Wednesday*
/ng/	**ng** as in *strong* **nk** as in *think*	**ngue** as in *tongue*	**ngg** as in *mahjongg* **nx** as in *anxiety*
/p/	**p** as in *pig* **pp** as in *guppy*	**ph** as in *shepherd*	**gh** as in *hiccough*
/r/	**r** as in *rare*	**rh** as in *rhythm* **rr** as in *terror* **rrh** as in *cirrhosis* **wr** as in *wring*	**rt** as in *mortgage* **l(o)** as in *colonel*
/s/	**c(e)** as in *celery* **c(i)** as in *city* **c(y)** as in *fancy* **s** as in *slime* **ss** as in *brass*	**ps** as in *pseudonym* **sc** as in *science* **st** as in *listen* **sw** as in *sword* **z** as in *quartz*	**sch** as in *schism*–2nd **sth** as in *isthmus*
/sh/	**c(i)** as in *suspicion* **sh** as in *shoe* **s(i)** as in *vision* **ss(i)** as in *mission* **t(i)** as in *gumption*	**c(e)** as in *oceanic* **ch** as in *chandelier* **s(u)** as in *sugar* **sch(i)** as in *schism* **sc(i)** as in *conscience* **s(e)** as in *nauseous* **ss(u)** as in *tissue*	**che** as in *cache* **chs(i)** as in *fuchsia* **psh** as in *pshaw* **zh** as in *pirozhki*
/t/	**t** as in *tiger* **tt** as in *cattle*	**bt** as in *debt* **ed** as in *vanished* **pt** as in *pterodactyl* **th** as in *thyme*	**cht** as in *yacht* **ct** as in *indict*

SOUND Consonant Sounds	SPELLINGS		
	Common	Less Common	Oddball
/v/	v as in *van*	f as in *of* lv(e) as in *calve*	
/w/	(q)u as in *quality* w as in *wet* wh as in *who*	(g)u as in *language* o as in *once* (s)u as in *suave* ui as in *cuisine*	
/y/	y as in *yum*	i as in *alleluia*	j as in *hallelujah*
/z/	z as in *zebra*	s as in *his* s(e) as in *turquoise* ss as in *scissors* x as in *xylophone* zz as in *buzz*	cz as in *czar* thes as in *clothes* ts as in *tsar*
/zh/	s(i) as in *decision* s(u) as in *unusual*	g(e) as in *garage* z(u) as in *azure*	g(i) as in *regime* t(i) as in *equation*

BRAIN TICKLERS
Set # 6

Choose 20 different spellings from the chart. Look up each of the example words in the dictionary to find out what language it came from originally. What conclusions can you draw?

(Answers are on page 31.)

The sound/sight strategy

Here's an overview of one strategy that can help you a lot. Let's call it the **sound/sight strategy** or **SSS**:

1. Look for visual patterns.

2. Look for sound patterns.

3. See how the sound patterns correspond to the visual patterns.

4. See if you can find a rule or rules that explain what's going on.

5. Look for more examples that support the rule.

6. Check your rule or rules for exceptions.

Here's a model for you. Look at this list:

bread | greed | head | leaf | neat | seed

Now check the patterns. Visually there are two patterns. And there are also two sound patterns.

VISUAL PATTERNS		SOUND PATTERNS	
ea	**ee**	**/ē/**	**/ĕ/**
bread	greed	greed	bread
head	seed	leaf	head
leaf		neat	
neat		seed	

But it is only by looking at the sound patterns AND the visual patterns together, that we can see what's really going on—**three** patterns:

SSS RESULTS		
/ē/		/ĕ/
ea	ee	ea
leaf	greed	bread
neat	seed	head

BRAIN TICKLERS
Set # 7

Extend the patterns of /ē/ and /ĕ/ by adding four words of your own choosing to each of the three categories.

(Answers are on page 31.)

23

LETTER PATTERNS

Earlier in this chapter, you saw that some sounds in English can be represented by quite a few letters and letter combinations. The chart beginning on page 16 looked at spelling from a sound point of view. Now, we're going to switch to a visual vantage point and look at the letter combinations to see which different sounds they can spell.

Some letter combinations for vowel sounds

Identical twins

Do you know any sets of identical twins? Have you ever called one of them by the wrong name? Chances are that if you did, you didn't get the answer you expected. Look below, and you'll see a set of identical quintuplets.

1. *i* spells /ă/ in *meringue*

2. *i* spells /ĭ/ in *bit*

3. *i* spells /ə/ in *pencil*

4. *i* spells /ē/ in *curious*

5. *i* spells /ī/ in *mild*

Now, what happens if you call one of them by the name belonging to another of them? In most cases, you just get a strange pronunciation of a word. But if you call *i* No. 2 by *i* No. 1's name, you know what happens? You hear the word *bat* instead of the word *bit*. And if you call *i* No. 2 by *i* No. 3's name, you hear the word *but* instead of the word *bit*. If you call *i* No. 2 by *i* No. 4's name, you hear *beat* or *beet* instead of *bit*. And if you call *i* No. 2 by *i* No. 5's name, you hear *bite* instead of *bit*. Whoops!

BRAIN TICKLERS
Set # 8

Use the chart on pages 15–21. For each letter or set of letters, write down the different sounds it can spell. Use the slashes and the symbols from the chart, plus a sample word. The sample word can be from the chart, or you can choose one of your own. If you're not sure, check it in the dictionary. A sample is given for you.

Letter(s)	Sound Symbol	Sample Word
a	/ă/	fabulous
a		
e		
i		
o		
u		
y		
ai		
au		
ea		
ei		
ie		
oo		
ou		
ow		
ui		
ear		

(Answers are on page 32.)

BRAIN TICKLERS
Set # 9

There's a saying used in teaching spelling: "When two vowels go walking, the first <u>one</u> does the <u>talking.</u>" Analyze the chart you made in Brain Tickler Set # 8. Find examples that support the saying. Find examples that don't support it. What conclusions can you draw?

(Answers are on page 33.)

Some letter combinations for consonant sounds

Party time

Have you ever been in this situation? You want to get together with two or three of your good friends, but they don't know each other, and you're not sure what will happen when they're together. Maybe they'll all try to assert themselves, and you'll feel like you're just a bunch of individuals, not a group. Maybe one will do all the talking, and the other will be silent. Or maybe you'll have a wonderful mixture in which every person contributes—a totally new experience. Any of these three things can happen when you combine more than one consonant letter.

Three possibilities

When we put consonant letters together, a variety of things can happen.

1. The consonant letters all keep "talking," and we get a **blend** in which each individual letter's sound can be heard.

Consonant letter combinations that make a blend:

BLENDS			
INITIAL BLEND			**FINAL BLEND**
bl as in *blue*	**fr** as in *fro*	**sp** as in *spun*	**ft** as in *heft*
cl as in *clue*	**gr** as in *grow*	**spr** as in *sprung*	**ld** as in *held*
fl as in *flu*	**pr** as in *prow*	**st** as in *stun*	**lt** as in *halt*
gl as in *glue*	**tr** as in *trowel*	**str** as in *straw*	**mp** as in *damp*
pl as in *plow*	**sc** as in *scan*	**sw** as in *swung*	**nd** as in *sand*
sl as in *slow*	**scr** as in *scram*	**tw** as in *twig*	**nt** as in *sent*
br as in *brow*	**sk** as in *skill*	**wh** as in *Whig*	**sk** as in *task*
cr as in *crow*	**sm** as in *smug*		**st** as in *test*
dr as in *drop*	**sn** as in *snug*		

2. At least one of the consonant letters is not heard (a **silent partner**). This can happen either when the consonant letters are the same or when different letters are included in the combination. Asterisks mark less frequent combinations.

Consonant letter combinations with a silent partner:

SILENT PARTNERS			
Double Letters	**Letter Combinations**		
bb as in *hobby*	**bt** as in *debt**	**kn** as in *knee*	**pt** as in *pterodactyl*
cc as in *acclaim* (not access)	**cch** as in *saccharine**	**lh** as in *lhasa apso*	**rh** as in *rhythm*
dd as in *daddy*	**chm** as in *drachm**	**lk** as in *walk*	**rrh** as in *cirrhosis*
ff as in *taffy*	**cht** as in *yacht**	**lm** as in *calm*	**rt** as in *mortgage**
gg as in *baggy*	**ct** as in *indict**	**ln** as in *kiln*–2nd	**sc** as in *science*
kk as in *trekked**	**ck** as in *clock*	**lv(e)** as in *calve*	**sch** as in *schism**–2nd
ll as in *hilly*	**dg(e)** as in *judge*	**mb** as in *lamb*	**st** as in *listen**
mm as in *yummy*	**dg(i)** as in *lodging*	**mn** as in *mnemonic* /n/	**sth** as in *isthmus**
nn as in *bunny*	**dn** as in *Wednesday**	**mn** as in *limn* /m/	**sw** as in *sword*
pp as in *happy*	**ft** as in *often*	**nd** as in *handsome**	**tch** as in *watch*
rr as in *hurry*	**gh** as in *ghost*	**ph** as in *shepherd*	**th** as in *thyme*
ss as in *sissy*	**gm** as in *diaphragm**	**pn** as in *pneumonia*	**ts** as in *tsar*
tt as in *chatty*	**gn** as in *gnaw*	**ps** as in *pseudonym*	**wh** as in *who*
zz as in *fizzy*	**kh** as in *khaki**	**psh** as in *pshaw**	**wr** as in *wring*

3. The consonant letter combination makes a new sound that neither can make alone (**digraph**).

Consonant letter combinations with a new sound (digraphs):

DIGRAPHS	
ch as in *chimp* /ch/	**sh** as in *shoe* /sh/
cz as in *Czech* /ch/	**tch** as in *watch* (digraph with silent partner) /ch/
gh as in *hiccough* /p/	**th** (voiced) as in *than* /th/
ng as in *strong* /ng/	**th** (unvoiced) as in *thanks* /th/
ph as in *photo* /f/	

Voiced and *unvoiced* have specialized meanings here. They refer to a distinction in the way a sound is produced. When you pronounce voiced sounds, your vocal chords vibrate. When you pronounce unvoiced sounds, they don't. Put your fingers gently on the front of your throat and say the following pairs of sounds, and you'll feel it:

Voiced Sounds	Unvoiced Sounds
/z/	/s/
/g/	/k/
/v/	/f/
/d/	/t/
/b/	/p/
/j/	/ch/

Now try saying *the* (voiced) and *thread* (unvoiced). Do you hear and feel the difference?

BRAIN TICKLERS
Set # 10

1. Write five words that contain a blend and are not in the blend chart.

2. Write five words that contain a silent partner and are not in the silent partner chart.

3. Write five words that contain a consonant digraph that are not in the digraph chart.

(Answers are on page 34.)

BRAIN TICKLERS—
THE ANSWERS

Set # 3, page 6

1. Answers will vary depending on the dictionaries and the words chosen. Here is a possible set of responses:

   Merriam Webster's 11th edition spellings

clearheaded	percent	teenage
cornflakes	retro-rocket	

2. Answers will vary depending on the dictionary or dictionaries chosen. Here is a possible response:

boogieman	boogeyman	bogeyman
boogyman	bogyman	

Set # 4, page 9

Answers will vary depending on which word you decide to spell and which spelling variants you use. One possible response is:

Oklahoma spelled Auquelliouhoughmmi.
Explanation:
au as in *chauvinist*   **iou** as in *anxious*   **mm** as in *Mommy*
que as in *oblique*   **h** as in *hamburger*   **i** as in *pencil*
ll as in *llama*   **ough** as in *though*

Set # 5, page 10

The words will vary. Possible responses include:
1. m**a**d   comrade, salve, laugh
2. b**i**t   marriage, business, guilty, gym
3. m**e**   meal, sneeze, treat, peat, Pete, ski, marine, receive, grieve, silly
4. n**o**   beau, stole, soap, toe, flow
5. lea**f**   scaffold, photograph, trough
6. **sh**oe   ocean, chamois, vision, mission, nation, sugar
7. **t**iger   rattle, Ptolemy, flashed, Thai, debtor, yacht, indict

Set # 6, page 21

Answers will vary. Possible responses include:

azure Persian   **knee** Old English   **slime** Old English
bouquet Old French   **meringue** French   **soufflé** Latin
buzz Middle English   **pneumonia** Greek   **sword** Old English
camel Semitic   **rhyme** Greek   **thyme** Greek
chandelier Latin   **rhythm** Greek   **women** Old English
fuchsia New Latin   **schism** Greek   **yacht** Middle German
garage Frankish   **science** Latin

Possible conclusion: From this sampling, the English language seems to have "inherited" many words from Greek, Old English, and Latin, and some (but fewer) from Persian, Frankish, French, Semitic, and German.

Set # 7, page 23

Possible responses:
Long *e* /ē/ spelled ea: heat, beat, seat, treat, sheaf, read (present tense), team, scream, dream, cheat
Long *e* /ē/ spelled ee: greet, feed, speed, need, heed, freed, parakeet, sleet, seem, skeet, creed
Short *e* /ĕ/ spelled ea: thread, tread, dead, read (past tense), lead (the metal), ahead, dread

Set # 8, page 25

Letter(s)	Sound Symbol	Sample Word
a	/ă/ /ĕ/ /ĭ/ /ə/ /ā/ /ē/	bat any portage balloon favor bologna
e	/ĕ/ /ĭ/ /ŭ/ /ə/ /ā/ /ē/	bet English them concentration rodeo–2nd me
i	/ă/ /ĭ/ /ə/ /ē/ /ī/	meringue bit pencil curious mild
o	/ĭ/ /ŭ/ /ə/ /ŏŏ/ /ō/ /ōō/	women done prison woman no to
u	/ĕ/ /ĭ/ /ŭ/ /ə/ /ŏŏ/ /ōō/ /yōō/	bury busy but circus bull Ruth human
y	/ĭ/ /ē/ /ī/	abyss happy my
ai	/ă/ /ĕ/ /ə/ /ā/ /ī/	plaid said captain mail Thailand

Letter(s)	Sound Symbol	Sample Word
au	/ă/ /ō/	laugh chauvinist
ea	/ĕ/ /ā/ /ē/	bread great peal
ei	/ĕ/ /ā/ /ē/ /ī/	leisure veil receive stein
ie	/ĕ/ /ē/ /ī/	friend thief lie
oo	/ŭ/ /o͝o/ /ō/ /o͞o/	flood wood brooch soon
ou	/u/ /ə/ /o͝o/ /ō/ /o͞o/ /ou/	trouble generous could soul you cloud
ow	/ō/ /ou/	mow frown
ui	/ĭ/ /o͞o/	build suit
ear	/âr/ /ûr/ /îr/	pear learn dear

Set # 9, page 26

It's true when *ai* spells /ā/; when *ea* spells /ĕ/ or /ē/; when *ei* spells /ē/; when *ie* spells /ī/; when *ow* spells /ō/; and when *ui* spells /o͞o/. In all other cases it is not true. You may conclude that it has limited use and that it might be more confusing than helpful.

Set # 10, page 30

Answers will vary. Possible responses:

1.

BLENDS			
Initial			**Final**
bl as in *blossom*	**fr** as in *frontier*	**sp** as in *spit*	**ft** as in *left*
cl as in *clean*	**gr** as in *granola*	**spr** as in *spring*	**ld** as in *shield*
fl as in *flood*	**pr** as in *prune*	**st** as in *statue*	**lt** as in *salt*
gl as in *glade*	**tr** as in *trigonometry*	**str** as in *stream*	**mp** as in *damp*
pl as in *plaid*	**sc** as in *scamp*	**sw** as in *swift*	**nd** as in *kind*
sl as in *sleigh*	**scr** as in *scream*	**tw** as in *twilight*	**nt** as in *dent*
br as in *breakfast*	**sk** as in *skim*	**wh** as in *whale*	**sk** as in *ask*
cr as in *creep*	**sm** as in *smelly*		**st** as in *last*
dr as in *dragon*	**sn** as in *snare drum*		

2.

SILENT PARTNERS			
Double Letters		**Letter Combinations**	
bb as in *babble*	**mm** as in *hammer*	**dg(e)** as in *judge*	**ps** as in *psalm*
cc as in *raccoon*	**nn** as in *penny*	**ft** as in *soften*	**pt** as in *ptarmigan*
dd as in *waddle*	**pp** as in *sloppy*	**ght** as in *night*	**rh** as in *rhapsody*
ff as in *giraffe*	**rr** as in *ferry*	**gn** as in *gnarled*	**sc** as in *scenic*
gg as in *giggle*	**ss** as in *hiss*	**kn** as in *knight*	**st** as in *fasten*
kk as in *bookkeeper*	**tt** as in *cattle*	**lk** as in *chalk*	**tch** as in *latch*
ll as in *wall*	**zz** as in *fuzzy*	**lm** as in *balmy*	**wh** as in *when*–2nd
		mb as in *plumber*	**wr** as in *wrong*
		pn as in *pneumatic*	

3.

CONSONANT DIGRAPHS

ch as in *charm* /ch/	**tch** as in *latch* (digraph with silent partner) /ch/
ng as in *sing* /ng/	**th** (voiced) as in *that* /th/
ph as in *phonograph* /f/	**th** (unvoiced) as in *thumb* /th/
sh as in *sheep* /sh/	

Did you know that the letters *wh* beginning a word are pronounced /hw/ in many dialects? In fact, some words that begin w-h used to begin with the spelling h-w! *Whelp* used to be *hwelp*. *While* used to be *hwil*. Hwat do you think of that?

CHAPTER TWO

"Let's Start at the Very Beginning"

THREE-LETTER WORDS: "A VERY GOOD PLACE TO START"

Do you remember kindergarten and first grade? Often in early schooling, simple facts in mathematics and spelling are taught with the idea of family. There are number families like 2, 5, and 7 that you can put together in addition and subtraction problems. There are word families, too.

To begin with, there are some really big patterns that we can call *dynasties*. These are identified by the patterns of consonant and vowel letters that they contain. To show them, we use a capital *V* to represent a vowel letter and a capital *C* to represent a consonant letter.

In the area of three-letter words, we can find CCV words like *pry*, and VCC words like *ohm*. There are CVV words like *goo*, VVC words like *aah*, and VCV words like *axe*. Just for review, we're going to spend a little time with three-letter word families that fit the pattern: consonant letter-vowel letter-consonant letter (CVC).

The kiddle in the middle

Having just three letters in a CVC dynasty word certainly narrows the possibilities for letter combinations. For example, no blends or diagraphs are possible. But wait! Can you think of ANY three letter CVC words that have a *y* in the middle? No? Well, there are at least two words—*gyp* and *gym*—but the possibilities just got even fewer. There just aren't that many things you can do with only three letters. But what you CAN do is worth exploring.

Group 1—The rhyming group

First, let's define one group of three-letter words and then hunt for families that fit.

> Three-letter-word Group 1 is a collection of three-letter words that have the same middle letter and the same final letter. Most of the words in each family of this group rhyme with each other.

An example of a family in this group is: *bun, fun, gun, Hun* (as in Attila), *nun, pun, run, sun.*

Notice how the list goes in alphabetical order? The easiest way to find members of a family is to go through the alphabet and try each letter on the front of the word to see if it fits. Also notice that proper nouns are allowed into the family. So are weird words. If you're doing the *it* family, you can include *zit.* Is there a family for *ez?* You bet. *Pez* (those little candies) and *fez* (a felt hat worn in eastern Mediterranean countries) will make a family for *ez*, if anyone asks you. The only rule is, if you're working with others, don't include any words that would offend them or show disrespect.

Can you think of any two three-letter words that have the same two last letters, but do NOT rhyme?

HINT: If this happens, it's usually because the vowel sound in the two words is different.

How about *cut* and *put?*

BRAIN TICKLERS
Set # 11

So who has the biggest family in Group 1? I'll give you a hint: families like *ez* are minuscule (really small) compared with some families you can find. So here's a challenge: What's the biggest family you can find in Group 1? On your mark, get set, go! Hint: If you aren't sure whether the letters you've put together make a word, check the biggest dictionary you can find. (The bigger the dictionary, the more words are in it—and yours might be there, too!)

(Answers are on page 52.)

Group 2—New beginnings

Are you ready for the next group? This group of words all begin with the same letters, but end with a different letter.

> Three-letter-word Group 2 is a collection of three-letter words that have the same initial letter and the same middle letter.

BRAIN TICKLERS
Set # 12

This may be harder to do, but give it a whirl—what's the largest family you can find for Group 2?

(Answers are on page 53.)

Family trees

In all your years of using the English language, you've probably learned some things about English that you don't even realize. See if these conclusions match your experiences in this chapter:

1. The letters x, q, y, c, and z are like distant cousins eight times removed—you hardly ever see them in three-letter words. Can you add other letters to this list?

2. The letter u is like an uncle who lives a few hours away—he appears only when he happens to be in town, less often than a, e, i, and o.

MORE ABOUT CONSONANT LETTER BLENDS AND DIGRAPHS

Initial digraphs and blends

The musketeers and the molecules

Imagine a CVC word with one or two extra consonant letters in front of it. Now you've got a CCVC word or a CCCVC word. The two or three consonant letters at the beginning of these words can fit into two different categories that we already met on page 39.

1. They can form a **blend,** in which you hear the sound of each letter one right after the other, like the first two letters of *blend: bl.*

   A blend is like the Three Musketeers: each one of them has his identity as a musketeer, and yet, when you see them together, you're still aware of their individual personalities. Try saying these blends to yourself: *st, tw, nd, cr.*

2. Or they can form a **digraph,** which, you may remember, we're using to refer to any group of two or three consonant letters representing a sound that is NOT the same as the sound of any of the individual consonant letters alone. Examples are *sh, th, ch.*

A digraph is like a molecule. When you put oxygen and hydrogen together, you get water, and its properties are different than the properties of either component. By joining things together, you have made something new and different.

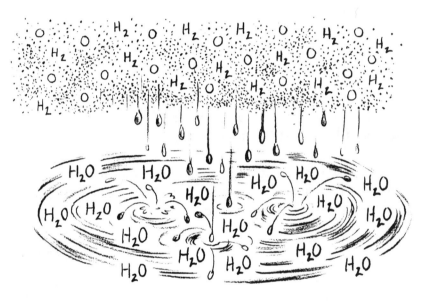

Note: They can also be a letter set with one or more silent part-ners. We'll learn more about those beginning on page 90.

BRAIN TICKLERS
Set # 13

Here is a collection of initial consonant blends and digraphs.

bl	*fl*	*pr*	*sm*	*sw*
br	*fr*	*sc*	*sn*	*th*
ch	*gl*	*sh*	*sp*	*tr*
cl	*gr*	*scr*	*spr*	*tw*
cr	*ph*	*sk*	*st*	*wh*
dr	*pl*	*sl*	*str*	

1. Say them aloud to decide which are which. Sort them into a group of blends and a group of digraphs.

2. Okay, now take the same list and sort it into some other groups that you think are useful. Explain in a sentence or two how you formed your groupings.

(Answers are on page 53.)

BRAIN TICKLERS
Set # 14

Read each list of words below. What do the words in each list have in common? They all are "molecule" words, and they all start with the same two letters. Sort each list into categories that make sense to you. Write a sentence or two explaining why you grouped the items the way you did. Then add three words to each category you made.

1. chalet chameleon Charlotte chauffeur cheese chef chemist cherry chicken chimpanzee choir cholesterol

2. thank-you thaw the then these they thief thistle though thunder

(Answers are on page 54.)

BRAIN TICKLERS
Set # 15

Here are some "musketeers": Make a list of five words that begin with each initial consonant letter blend listed below.

bl	*fl*	*pr*	*sm*	*str*
br	*fr*	*sc*	*sn*	*sw*
cl	*gl*	*scr*	*sp*	*tr*
cr	*gr*	*sk*	*spr*	*tw*
dr	*pl*	*sl*	*st*	*wh*

(Answers are on page 54.)

BRAIN TICKLERS
Set # 16

Using what you've learned so far, explain the group of initial consonant letters in each of the following words.

thrice   phrase   shrapnel   chrome

(Answers are on page 55.)

Final digraphs and blends

More musketeers and molecules

Imagine a CVC word with one or two extra consonant letters following it. Now you've got a CVCC word or a CVCCC word. The two or three consonant letters at the end can fit into the same two categories: blends ("musketeers") or digraphs ("molecules").

BRAIN TICKLERS
Set # 17

Take a look at this list of initial blends and digraphs. See if you can figure out which ones can also be final blends and digraphs. Make a list and write down a word for each one that works as an ending.

bl	fl	pr	sm	sw
br	fr	sc	sn	th
ch	gl	sh	sp	tr
cl	gr	scr	spr	tw
cr	ph	sk	st	wh
dr	pl	sl	str	

(Answers are on page 55.)

BRAIN TICKLERS
Set # 18

Now, using your memory (and a dictionary), try to think of some blends and digraphs that we haven't covered yet but that can appear at the end of words.

(Answers are on page 55.)

BRAIN TICKLERS
Set # 19

Take this list of final blends and digraphs and sort it into groups that you think are useful. Explain in a sentence or two how you formed your groupings.

ch	mp	ph	sk	th
ft	nd	rd	sp	ts
ld	ng	sc	st	tz
lt	nt	sh	tch	

(Answers are on page 55.)

BRAIN TICKLERS
Set # 20

The digraphs *tch* and *ch* both spell the sound /ch/ at the end of a word. Make a list of as many *tch* and *ch* words as you can think of. What patterns do you find in the middle of your words? Sort the list, not by the final digraph, but by the LETTERS BETWEEN the final digraph and the initial consonant letter, blend, or digraph (if there is one—if not, start with the vowel or two adjacent vowels closest to the final blend or digraph). Write a sentence or two explaining how you grouped the words.

(Answers are on page 55.)

BRAIN TICKLERS
Set # 21

Now, for each final blend and digraph listed below, write five words that use that ending.

ft	*nd*	*ph*	*sk*	*th*
ld	*ng*	*rd*	*sp*	*ts*
lt	*nk*	*sh*	*st*	*tz*
mp	*nt*			

(Answers are on page 55.)

BRAIN TICKLERS
Set # 22

Using what you've learned, explain the groups of final consonant letters in the following words. What kinds of groups are they?

depth   search   hearts   tenth   harsh

(Answers are on page 56.)

BRAIN TICKLERS—
THE ANSWERS

Set # 11, page 42

Some of the larger families of Group 1 include:

ED family	bed, fed, Jed, led, Ned, red, Ted, wed, zed (another name for the letter *z*) (9)
EW family	dew, few, hew, Jew, mew, new, pew, sew, yew (9)
OD family	cod, God, hod (holder for coal), mod, nod, pod, rod, sod (grass), Tod (9)
OP family	bop, cop, fop, hop, lop, mop, pop, sop, top (9)
UG family	bug, dug, hug, jug, lug, mug, pug, rug, tug (9)
AR family	bar, car, far, gar (a fish), jar, Lar (a Roman household god), mar, par, tar, war (10)
AT family	bat, cat, fat, hat, mat, pat, rat, sat, tat, vat (10)
IN family	bin, din, fin, gin, kin, pin, sin, tin, win, yin (Chinese: female cosmic principle, opposite of yang) (10)
IT family	bit, fit, git (British for a worthless person), hit, kit, lit, pit, sit, wit, zit (10)
OG family	bog, cog, dog, fog, hog, jog, log, nog (as in eggnog), pog (paper bottlecaps), tog (dress up) (10)

AN family	ban, can, Dan, fan, man, Nan, pan, ran, tan, van, wan (11)
AP family	cap, gap, lap, map, nap, pap, rap, sap, tap, yap, zap (11)
ET family	bet, get, jet, let, met, net, pet, set, vet, wet, yet (11)
OT family	cot, dot, got, hot, jot, lot, not, pot, rot, sot, tot, wot (British verb meaning "know") (12)
AD family	bad, cad, dad, fad, gad, had, lad, mad, pad, rad (a unit of radiation), sad, tad, wad (13)
EN family	Ben, den, fen (low land covered with water), hen, Jen, Ken, men, pen, sen (an Asian coin), ten, yen, wen (a cyst), Zen (13)
OW family	bow, cow, Dow (Jones average), how, low, mow, now, pow, row, sow, tow, vow, wow, yow (14)

Set # 12, page 43

PE family	ped, peg, pen, pep, per, pet, pew, Pez (8)
SA family	sad, sag, Sam, sap, sat, saw, sax, say (8)
SI family	sic, Sid, sin, sip, sir, Sis, sit, six (8)
SO family	sob, sod, Sol, son, sop, sot, sow, soy (8)
TA family	tab, tad, tag, tan, tap, tar, tat, tax (8)
CA family	cab, cad, Cal, can, cap, car, cat, caw, cay (a coral reef) (9)
MA family	Mac, mad, man, map, mar, mat, maw, Max, may (9)
PA family	pad, pal, Pam, pan, par, pat, paw, pax, pay (9)
WA family	WAC (Women's Army Corps), wad, WAF (Women in the Air Force), wag, wan, war, was, wax, way (9)
RA family	rad (dose of radiation), rag, rah, Raj (British rule in India), ram, ran, rap, rat, raw, ray (10)

Set # 13, page 46

1. **Blends:** *bl br cl cr dr fl fr gl gr pl pr sc scr sk sl sm sn sp spr st str sw tr tw wh*
   Digraphs: *ch ph sh th*

2. Answers may vary. Possible responses follow:
   three-letter blends: *scr, spr, str*
   blends with a /k/ sound: *cl, cr, sc, scr, sk*
   l-blends: *bl, cl, fl, gl, pl, sl*
   p-blends: *pl, pr, spr*
   r-blends: *br, cr, dr, fr, gr, pr, scr, spr, str, tr*
   s-blends: *sc, scr, sk, sl, sm, sn, sp, spr, st, str, sw*
   t-blends: *st, str, tr, tw*
   digraphs: *ch, ph, sh, th, wh*
   digraphs that can spell more than one sound: *ch, th*

Set # 14, page 47

Possible responses:
1. **ch sounds like /k/:** chameleon, chemist, choir, cholesterol
   ch sounds /sh/: chalet, Charlotte, chauffeur, chef
   ch sounds like /ch/: cheese, cherry, chicken, chimpanzee

   Additional words:
   ch sounds like /k/: choreography, cholera, chasm, chameleon, charisma
   ch sounds /sh/: Cheyenne, chateau, chaparral, chanticleer, chaise lounge
   ch sounds like /ch/: chess, cheddar, Chinese, chapter, chinchilla

2. **th sounds like /th/:** thank-you, thaw, thief, thistle, thunder
   th sounds like /th/: the, then, these, they, though

   Additional words:
   th sound like /th/: thick, thermometer, thrill, thesaurus, theater
   th sounds like /th/: thy, that, themselves, there, they'd

Set # 15, page 48

Answers will vary. Possible answers include:

bl	blond, blood, blimp, bloated, black
br	brown, brawny, bruised, brooding, Brahman
cl	clown, closet, cloister, cloudy, clunk
cr	crumpet, cruise, crooked, crocodile, Creole
dr	drip, drum, dreadful, dromedary, droll
fl	Florida, flippers, floral, flea, flowing
fr	Frisbee, fry, fraud, frazzled, frosting
gl	gloat, glad, glutton, gloaming, glacier
gr	green, grab, gruesome, grueling, gravel
pl	plunk, plank, plink, plumber, plywood
pr	predator, prune, prominent, pragmatic, prairie dog
sc	scattered, scapegoat, scuttle, scab, scone
scr	scram, scream, scrap, scrape, scrimshaw
sk	skunk, skim, skillet, skeleton, ski
sl	slam, slang, slippery, slap, sloop
sm	smash, smithereens, smuggle, smelly, smorgasbord
sn	sneeze, snort, snicker, sneer, snigger
sp	spell, spittoon, spawn, spangled, spider
spr	spring, sprightly, spruce, sprinkles, spray
st	stab, stirrup, stellar, staring, steal
str	stream, stripe, strobe, strum, strong
sw	swipe, sweet, swell, swagger, swing
tr	trivia, treehouse, trapper, triangular, tragedy
tw	twerp, tweet, twister, twirl, tweak
wh	(Note: Not everyone pronounces *wh* as a blend.) whale, wharf, what, where, why

Set # 16, page 48

They are all blends composed of a digraph and *r*.

Set # 17, page 49

ch peach
ph telegraph
sc disc

sh shush
sk disk
sm chasm

sp grasp
st forest
th forsooth

Set # 18, page 50

Possible answers:

ft	lt	nd	nt	tch
ld	mp	ng	rd	ts

Set # 19, page 50

Possible responses:
two blends or digraphs that make the same sound: sc/sk tch/ch tz/ts
digraph that makes two different sounds: ch
t blends: ft lt nt st ts tz
s blends: sc sk sp st ts
digraphs: ch ng ph sh tch th

Set # 20, page 51

Possible responses:
ch words with Vr: torch, perch, arch, birch, lurch
ch words with Vn: conch, bench, pinch, ranch, scrunch
ch words with V: rich, much, loch, attach
ch words with VV: pouch, peach, pooch, poach, screech
ch words with VVC: haunch, search
tch words with V: watch, witch, etch, Dutch, Scotch

Set # 21, page 51

ft   theft, raft, drift, aloft, tuft
ld   scald, held, gild, bold, guild
lt   halt, pelt, gilt, bolt, guilt
mp   damp, hemp, limp, chomp, bump
nd   wand, wend, wind, bond, cummerbund
ng   tang, zing, gong, lung, sling
nk   yank, fink, plonk, skunk, oink

nt   rant, accent, flint, don't, blunt
ph   graph, aleph, hieroglyph, humph, triumph
rd   weird, beard, bird, cord, curd
sh   ash, mesh, wish, gosh, blush
sk   mask, desk, risk, kiosk, rusk
sp   clasp, wisp, cusp, hasp, grasp
st   fast, fest, fist, cyst, dust
th   bath, Elizabeth, pith, sooth, truth
ts   gnats, bets, kits, plots, guts
tz   ersatz, klutz

Set # 22, page 52

depth   blend of *p* and digraph *th*
search   blend of *r* and digraph *ch*
hearts   blend of *r*, *t*, and *s*
tenth   blend of *n* and digraph *th*
harsh   blend of *r* and digraph *sh*

CHAPTER THREE

Vowel Sounds

SHORT VOWEL SOUNDS

A vowel is not what you think

The vowels in English are *a*, *e*, *i*, *o*, *u*, and sometimes *y*, right? Not quite! Remember, a vowel is not a letter—it's a sound during which air flows from your throat through and out of your mouth without being stopped. If the air is partially or completely cut off during a sound, then you've made a consonant sound.

The letters named above USUALLY represent vowel sounds. But there are exceptions. Sometimes letters we have come to think of as "vowels" may represent consonant sounds. For example, the letter *u* often represents the consonant sound /w/, as in the word *quiet*. And sometimes the letters we think of as consonants help to represent vowel sounds, as in the word *delight*, where the letters *i*, *g*, and *h* work together to display a vowel sound /ī/, according to one explanation.

We classify English vowel sounds into groups to make it easier to think and talk about them. Common groupings include: **short vowels, long vowels, r-controlled vowels,** and **diphthongs.** We are going to talk about each of these groups in separate sections to help you focus.

Introducing . . . (drumroll) the shorts

The letters *a, e, i, o,* and *u* each have a "short" form (short because they sound for a shorter time, so it's said). They are heard in the following words:

a cat   **e** bedbug   **i** iguana   **o** grasshopper   **u** butterfly

But wait! Stop! Hold everything! Let's rewind to *grasshopper.* Not everybody pronounces these sounds the same way. To understand more, try this experiment.

BRAIN TICKLERS
Set # 23

Say all of these words out loud to yourself. Make lists (as many as you need) to show the different vowel pronunciations you use when you say the bold-faced letters. Note: There is no right or wrong answer. Just divide the words into the categories YOU use.

all **awful** **bah** **bazaar** **bore** **bought**
call **caught** **caw** **chalk** **cod** **collar** **cot**
daughter **father** **frog** **gnaw** **guard**
guitar **heart** **honor** **horse** **knowledge**
laundry **lot** **pot** **quality** **salami** **sauce**
sergeant **stalk** **taut** **tot** **wharf**

1. Now look at the pronunciation lists on pages 73 to 74 from *The American Heritage Dictionary.* Compare and contrast your groups with the dictionary's groups. What observations can you make? Now compare your answers with the *Merriam Webster's* groupings.

2. Now classify each of your groups according to the spellings of the vowel sound. Briefly explain your classifications.

(Answers are on page 73.)

Dia-who?

People in different parts of the United States (and elsewhere) who speak English pronounce words somewhat differently, depending on the regional **dialect** that they speak. A dialect is a subset of a language, usually confined to a particular region. There are three main dialect areas in the United States: Northern, Southern, and Midland. But the differences in pronunciation are so specific that a language specialist could listen to you and tell whether you are from the Northern Middle West; New England; Chicago; the Central Atlantic Seaboard; Gary, Indiana; the Southern Coast; New York City; and so on. (African American English is an example of a dialect that is NOT regionalized.) No particular dialect is better than any other dialect, although some may be more popular than others, or people may CLAIM that theirs is superior.

The differences in dialect are noticeable when you listen to the way words like *father* and *hot* are pronounced. In any dictionary you check, you will probably find some words with /ä/ that you pronounce /ŏ/ and vice versa. And dictionaries are by no means in agreement about the number one spelling for these words.

Compared to this, /ă/, /ĕ/, and /ĭ/ are EASY.

BRAIN TICKLERS
Set # 24

1. For the sounds /ă/, /ĕ/, and /ĭ/, find as many different spellings as you can and write a word that has each spelling. You may use the chart on page 16 for help, but for every spelling you include from the chart, add another word in English that has that spelling and isn't on the chart, if you can.

2a. Group the /ă / spellings you found into categories that make sense to you. Write a sentence or two explaining your categories.

b. Now do the same for /ĕ /.

c. Time to repeat the procedure for /ĭ /.

(Answers are on page 74.)

Time out for an explanation

To prepare for talking about short *u*, we need to introduce a couple of terms. Don't worry! You've probably heard these before. The first one is **syllable.** A syllable is a vowel sound, either by itself or with the preceding and following consonant sounds. The word *syllable* has three distinct syllables: syl la ble. How many syllables in *antidisestablishmentarianism?* Twelve (check it out).

All stressed out

Do you know what a **stressed syllable** is? No, it's not one that's had a really hard day. When we say words, we usually say one part more loudly than any other part. That's the primary stress. In the word *metropolis*, we say *trop* louder than the rest. That's the primary stress. In the word *discombobulate* (it means to upset something or mess something up), we say *bob* the loudest, but *dis* and *late*, although softer than *bob*, are louder than *com* and *u*. That's called secondary stress. Try saying it yourself.

One way to represent stress is with little stress flags. Primary stress has a thicker, darker flag than secondary stress. Dictionaries use this system.

O´ver worked´

Uhhhhhhh

When the sound of short *u* appears in a word in a stressed syllable like butterfly, we call it "short *u*." But in a lot of English
words, a sound like short *u* appears in unstressed syllables.
When such a sound appears in an UN-stressed syllable, we call
the sound a **schwa** and represent it with this symbol: ə.

The word *schwa* comes from a Syriac word meaning "equal"—
maybe because many different sounds are kind of "equalized" into
one sound (more or less) in unstressed syllables. Here are some
examples that will show you how sounds are equalized:

> *methodical* (short o /ŏ/) → *method* (schwa /ə/)
> *medicinal* (short i /ĭ/) → *medicine* (schwa /ə/)
> *telegraphy* (short e /ĕ/) → *telegraph* (schwa /ə/)
> *tyrannical* (short a /ă/) → *tyrant* (schwa /ə/)
> *combine* (long i /ī/) → *combination* (schwa /ə/)

Get the idea?

If you try saying the words with the
schwa sounds, you may notice that your pronunciation of that sound is not exactly the same in
all the words. That's the way English works: Sounds are
affected by their context: the letters before and after them,
whether they appear in a stressed or unstressed syllable,
and so on.

BRAIN TICKLERS
Set # 25

Hidden in this word search are the names of nine musical instruments. Three of the instruments have only a short u sound /ŭ/. Four of them have only a schwa /ə/ sound. Two of them have both a short u /ŭ/ AND a schwa /ə/. Words are horizontal, vertical, or diagonal and may be forward or backward. Find the words and group them in the proper categories.

```
S  I  U  S  R  I  P  E  C  O  R  O  C  U  P  T  R  M
S  C  R  D  P  E  T  O  C  L  C  R  D  L  E  E  E  A
A  L  M  I  O  R  D  X  X  T  A  O  U  O  T  N  C  D
N  O  I  S  S  U  C  R  E  P  U  L  L  R  U  I  O  O
O  M  R  U  S  O  B  P  O  N  E  T  C  I  N  R  R  U
H  U  U  I  D  D  M  L  I  C  P  O  I  O  M  A  D  B
P  R  A  L  N  U  O  D  E  H  E  X  M  D  I  L  I  C
O  D  C  L  R  M  B  T  O  B  X  R  E  C  C  C  O  I
S  S  I  T  C  U  E  C  U  S  A  B  R  E  I  R  U  N
S  S  N  T  O  N  C  O  R  H  U  S  E  R  S  X  O  P
X  A  O  D  E  N  O  H  P  O  X  A  S  U  N  E  T  M
A  B  N  I  R  P  H  O  D  D  U  L  C  O  R  I  O  U
```

(Answers are on page 75.)

BRAIN TICKLERS
Set # 26

1. Sort these short vowel words into groups that make sense to you. Write a sentence or two explaining your categories.

   business   calf   dog   dread   necessary
   giraffe   gnat   guest   guild   marriage
   twit

2. Compare these word pairs in which some of the letters are identical. What do you find?

   business/buster
   calf/halt
   dog/ogre
   dread/mead
   necessary/far
   guest/glue
   guild/ennui (This means "boredom"; it's pronounced (ŏn-wē′).)

3. Sort these short a /ă/ words into groups that make sense to you. Write a sentence or two explaining your categories.

   babble   bad   baffle   bag   battle   can   cattle   haggle   ham
   hassle   man   paddle   rat   stammer   zap

4. Now add short e /ĕ/, short i /ĭ/, short o /ŏ/, and short u /ŭ/ words to each category you made, if possible.

(Answers are on page 76).

LONG VOWEL SOUNDS

O, i long 4 u

In this section we are going to talk about the sounds called long *a* /ā/, *e* /ē/, *i* /ī/, *o* /ō/, and *u* /ū/. The long vowel sounds are the sounds that you hear when you say the names of the letters *a*, *e*, *i*, *o*, and *u* PLUS the sound /o͞o/ without the /y/ sound. Even though long *u* has a consonant sound /y/ at the beginning, for example, in the word *cute*, we still call it a vowel sound. As you know, both from your own experience and from the chart in Chapter 1 (page 16 and following), long vowel sounds are not always spelled with the letter whose name you hear. In fact, some of them have some pretty strange spellings.

Cuuuuul man!

I think you mean coooool.

Taste your vowels

We usually don't think too much about how vowels feel in
our mouths. But if you try these experiments, you'll learn
something.

BRAIN TICKLERS
Set # 27

1. Say *beet, boot, bait, boat, bite*. Notice how
   your lips move in and out. Describe what
   happens.

2. Say *bait, boat*, and *bite*, one at a time, and
   try to hold the vowel sound for a long time.
   Describe what happens.

3. Say the names of the letters *e, a, i*. How
   does your mouth position change as you
   move through the three vowel sounds?

4. Say the short vowels /ă/, /ĕ/, /ĭ/, /ŏ/, /ŭ/. Describe how your
   mouth changes. Now say the long vowels /ā/, /ē/, /ī/, /ō/, /ū/.
   Describe how your mouth changes. How were the two sets
   different?

(Answers are on page 76.)

Now let's see if you can pick out the long vowels by sound (and
feel).

BRAIN TICKLERS
Set # 28

Sort this list into words with short vowel sounds and words with long vowel sounds.

bread	seat
flat	flavor
oven	to
he	met
lemonade	comrade
crumb	truth
gauge	laugh
people	leopard
human	but
bit	wild
soon	flood
gym	my
you	trouble

(Answers are on page 77.)

Caution—Major Mistake Territory!

The short and long vowels are spelled the same way in each pair of words, so watch out!

BRAIN TICKLERS
Set # 29

Use the symbols V for vowel letter and C for consonant letter (in combination if necessary) to show patterns of spelling for long vowels /ā/, /ē/, /ī/, /ō/, /yōō/, and /ōō/ that occur in the words in Set # 28. Show the pattern for the entire syllable that the long vowel appears in. Then brainstorm to find other patterns of two to six vowel and consonant letters that can convey syllables with long vowel sounds. Next to each pattern you identify, write a word that has the same pattern.

(Answers are on page 77.)

BRAIN TICKLERS
Set # 30

For the sounds of long a, e, i, o, and the two forms of long u (/yōō/ and /ōō/), find as many different spellings as you can and write a word that has that spelling. You may use the chart on pages 16–18 for help, but for every spelling you include from the chart, also include a different word in English that has that spelling, if you can find one.

(Answers are on page 77.)

BRAIN TICKLERS
Set # 31

Homophones are words that sound the same but are spelled differently, like *meat* and *meet*. Here is a list of some words with a long vowel sound, each of which has at least one homophone. Write the homophone(s) for each.

1. ale
2. isle
3. bail
4. base
5. Bea
6. beech
7. bow
8. boulder
9. bold
10. breech
11. brake
12. brood
13. bridle
14. buy
15. sealing
16. cheep
17. choose
18. site
19. creek
20. cruise
21. daze
22. due
23. dye
24. dough
25. does (several female deer)

(Answers are on page 79.)

BRAIN TICKLERS
Set # 32

Read the definitions separated by semicolons. Write a set of long vowel homophones that matches each set of definitions.

1. a person who colors cloth; disastrous

2. the overhang at the edge of a roof; periods between dusk and night

3. the organ of sight; first person singular pronoun; how a sailor says "yes"

4. when a person loses consciousness; a move designed to trick someone

5. destiny; a celebration

6. a small insect that often lives on dogs; to run away

7. lets go from prison; to be very cold; a decorative band around the wall of a room

8. a chicken made especially for cooking in deep fat; a brother in a religious order

9. the pace of a horse; an entrance through a wall

10. to create fine powder out of hard cheese; wonderful and outstanding

(Answers are on page 79.)

BRAIN TICKLERS
Set # 33

How many sets of homophones can you find with different spellings of the same long vowel? (No fair using homophones used in Brain Ticklers Sets # 31 and # 32.)

Get 10 and you're good.
Get 20 and you're an expert.
Get 30 or more and you're out of this world!

(Answers are on page 80.)

BRAIN TICKLERS—
THE ANSWERS

Set # 23, page 60

1. Here are some possible responses based on two dictionaries:

	American Heritage	Merriam Webster's
Group 1	all awful bore bought call caught caw chalk daughter frog gnaw horse laundry sauce stalk taut wharf	all awful bought call caught caw chalk daughter frog gnaw horse laundry sauce stalk taut wharf
Group 2	bah bazaar father guard guitar heart salami sergeant	bore

Group 3	cod collar cot honor knowledge lot pot quality tot	bah bazaar cod collar cot father guard guitar heart honor knowledge lot pot quality salami sergeant tot

Answers will vary. You might conclude that pronunciation of these closely related sounds is highly irregular and hard to categorize.

2. Possible response (based on *American Heritage* groupings):
Most short *o* words are spelled with an *o*, and most are in CVC words.
/ô/ can be spelled *a, aw, o_e, ough, augh, aw, al, o, au.*
/ä/ can be spelled *ah, aa, a, a(r), ea(r), e(r).*

Set # 24, page 62

1. Possible responses:

short a

a rat	*a_ _e* dance	*al* calf
au aunt	*i* timbre	

short e

a many	*ai* again	*e* debt
ea sweat	*ei* heifer	*eo* jeopardy
u burial	*ue* guest	

short i

a_e courage	*e* pretty	*i* snit
ia marriage	*u* business	*ui* built
y crystal		

2. Possible responses:

a. /ă/ **One letter spellings: a, i**   **Multiple letter spellings: a_e, ai, au**

a as in *rat*	**a_ _e** as in *dance*
i as in *timbre*	**al** as in *calf*
	au as in *aunt*

b. /ĕ/ **Spellings with e in them: e, ea, ei, eo**   **Spellings without e in them: a, ai, u**

e as in *debt*	**eo** as in *jeopardy*	**a** as in *many*
ea as in *sweat*		**ai** as in *again*
ei as in *heifer*		**u** as in *burial*

c. /ĭ/ **Spellings with i in them:**
i, ia, ui

Spellings without i in them:
a_e, e, u, y

i as in *snit*
ia as in *marriage*
ui as in *built*

a_e as in *courage*   **u** as in *business*
e as in *pretty*   **y** as in *crystal*

Set # 25, page 65

```
S  I  U  S  R  I  P  E  C  O  R  O  C  U  P  T  R  M
S  C  R  D  P  E  T  O  C  L  C  R  D  L  E  E  E  A
A  L  M  I  O  R  D  X  X  T  A  O  U  O  T  N  C  D
N  O  I  S  S  U  C  R  E  P  U  L  L  R  U  I  O  O
O  M  R  U  S  O  B  P  O  N  E  T  C  I  N  R  R  U
H  U  U  I  D  D  M  L  I  C  P  O  I  O  M  A  D  B
P  R  A  L  N  U  O  D  E  H  E  X  M  D  I  L  I  C
O  D  C  L  R  M  B  T  O  B  X  R  E  C  C  C  O  I
S  S  I  T  C  U  E  C  U  S  A  B  R  E  I  R  U  N
S  S  N  T  O  N  C  O  R  H  U  S  E  R  S  X  O  P
X  A  O  D  E  N  O  H  P  O  X  A  S  U  N  E  T  M
A  B  N  I  R  P  H  O  D  D  U  L  C  O  R  I  O  U
```

short *u* /ŭ/: tr**u**mpet, d**ou**ble bass, bass dr**u**m
schwa /ə/: harmonic**a**, sax**o**phone, clarin**e**t, record**e**r
both: perc**u**ssi**o**n, d**u**lcimer

Set # 26, page 66

1. Possible responses:
   short i words: business (spelled *u* and *e*), guild (spelled *ui*), marriage (spelled *ia*), twit (spelled *i*), giraffe (spelled *i*)
   short a words: calf (spelled *al*), gnat (spelled *a*), giraffe (spelled *a_e*)
   short e words: necessary (spelled *e* and *a*), dread (spelled *ea*), guest (spelled *ue*)

2. In each case the identical letters represent different sounds in the two different words.

3. Possible responses:
   CVC words with short vowels: bad, bag, can, ham, man, rat, zap
   words with short vowels followed by a double consonant: babble, baffle, battle, cattle, haggle, hassle, paddle, stammer

4. **CVC words with short vowels:** fed, lid, cod, mud
   words with short vowels followed by a double consonant: tessellate, hiss, bottle, snuggle

Set # 27, page 68

Your descriptions may be a little different than these, but you'll get the general idea:

1. Lips are pulled back as in a grin for *bee, bait,* and *bite*; rounded and forward for *boot* and *boat.*

2. You cannot hold the vowel sound because it's actually made up of two different sounds. The technical term for this (in case you don't remember) is *diphthong.* It may also be called a *vowel glide.*

3. It opens progressively wider for each vowel.

4. Answers will vary. For the short vowels, the sound seems to come from about the same place in the back of my mouth, but my lips and jaw move around to change the vowel. For the long vowels, the sound seems to come from farther forward in my mouth, and just like for the long vowels, my lips and jaw move around to change the vowel. The short vowels and long vowels seem to be in different places in my mouth.

Set # 28, page 69

Short: bread, flat, oven, met, comrade, crumb, laugh, leopard, but, bit, flood, gym, trouble

Long: seat, flavor, to, he, lemonade, truth, gauge, people, human, wild, soon, my, you

Set # 29, page 70

Here are the words from Set # 28:

seat CVVC	**truth** CCVCC	**human** CV
flavor CCV	**gauge** CVVCV	**wild** CVCC
my, to, he CV	**you, people** CVV	**soon** CVVC
lemonade VCV		

Here are words and patterns arranged in increasing length (answers will vary):

CV my	**CVCC** comb	**CVVCe** mayonnaise
VC I'm	**CVVC** coat	**CVVVC** Seoul
CVV jay	**CVVV** beau	**CCVCC** brush
CCV cry	**CVCe** cone	**CCVCCC** bright
VVV eau (it comes from the French word for "water")	**CVCCe** waste	
	CVVCC heist	

Set # 30, page 70

Reminder: I have used the term *Oddball* to refer to a rare spelling, maybe even a unique spelling in English. I have not been able to find a definitive list of all possible English spellings for each sound.

Long a /ā/

a as in *flavor*
a_e as in *tame*
a_ _e as in *taste*
ae as in *sundae*
ai as in *rain*
ai_e as in *plaice*
(It's a fish, and Rudyard Kipling mentions it in the story "How the Whale Got His Throat.")

aigh ODDBALL
Can you think of anything besides *straight?*
au ODDBALL
Can you think of anything besides *gauge?*
ay as in br*ay*
é as in *café*
e_e as in *fete*
ea as in *steak*

ee as in *toupee*
ei as in *sheik*
eigh as in *sleigh*
et as in *croquet*
ey as in *obey*

VOWEL SOUNDS

Long e /ē/

ae as in *aegis*
ay as in *hurray*
e as in *aborigine*
e_e as in *athlete*
ea as in *pea*
ea_e as in *grease*
ee as in *employee*
ei as in *protein*

eo ODDBALL
Can you think of
anything besides
people?
ey as in *monkey*
i as in *kiwi*
i_e as in
automobile
ie as in *achieve*

is as in *ambergris*
(second pronun-
ciation from
*Merriam Web-
ster's Collegiate
Dictionary*)
oe as in *Phoebe*
y as in *uncanny*

Long i /ī/

ai as in *naiad* and
Shanghai—and
that's it, accord-
ing to Edward
Carney in *A
Survey of
English
Spelling*
ais Carney says
aisle is the
only English
word with this
spelling.

ay as in *cayenne*
(very rare
spelling)
ei as in
kaleidoscope
eigh as in *sleight*
ey as in *geyser*
(very rare
spelling)
i as in *alibi*
i_e as in *crime*
ie as in *pie*
igh as in *knight*

is as in *isle*
oy ODDBALL
Can you think of
anything besides
coyote?
ui_e ODDBALL
Can you think of
anything besides
guide?
y as in *wry*
ye as in *rye*
y_e as in *thyme*

Long o /ō/

au as in *chauffeur*
eau as in *bureau*
eo ODDBALL
Can you think of
anything besides
yeoman?
ew ODDBALL
Can you think of
anything besides
sew?
o as in *burro*
o_e as in *nose*

oa as in *hoax*
oe as in *toe*
oh as in *Shiloh*
ol as in *molt*
ou as in *boulder*
ough as in *dough*
ow as in *bungalow*
owe ODDBALL
Can you think of
anything besides
owe(s)?

Note: Here are
some other
oddball /o/
spellings, just
for you:
aoh—as in
pharaoh
eou—as in *Seoul*
oo—as in
Roosevelt

Long u /ōō/

eu as in
  rheumatism
ew as in *grew*
ho as in *whom*
o as in *tomb*
oo as in *raccoon*
o_e as in *lose*

oe as in *shoe*
  (very rare)
ou as in *croup*
ough ODDBALL
  Can you think of
  anything besides
  through?
u as in *gnu*

u_e as in *prune*
ue as in *glue*
ui as in *bruise*
wo ODDBALL Can
  you think of
  anything besides
  two?

Long u /yōō/

eau ODDBALL
  Can you think
  of anything
  besides *beauty?*

ew as in *nephew*
iew as in *view*
u as in *unity*

ue as in *argue*
u_e as in *huge*

Set # 31, page 71

Possible responses:

1. ail
2. aisle
3. bale
4. bass
5. be, bee
6. beach
7. beau
8. bolder
9. bowled
10. breach
11. break
12. brewed
13. bridal
14. by
15. ceiling
16. cheap
17. chews
18. cite, sight
19. creak
20. crews
21. days
22. dew
23. die
24. doe
25. doze

Set # 32, page 72

1. dyer, dire
2. eaves, eves
3. eye, I, aye
4. faint, feint
5. fate, fete
6. flea, flee
7. frees, freeze, frieze
8. fryer, friar
9. gait, gate
10. grate, great

Set # 33, page 73

1. gale, Gail
2. greys, graze
3. groan, grown
4. grosser, grocer
5. guys, guise
6. heal, heel
7. hew, hue
8. higher, hire
9. hoes, hose
10. knave, nave
11. knead, need
12. knew, new
13. know, no
14. knows, nose
15. liar, lyre
16. load, lode
17. loan, lone
18. made, maid
19. male, mail
20. mane, main
21. maze, maize
22. moat, mote
23. mooed, mood
24. mowed, mode
25. night, knight
26. owed, ode
27. paced, paste
28. pail, pale
29. pain, pane
30. peace, piece
31. peak, peek, pique
32. peal, peel
33. pi, pie
34. plaice, place
35. plane, plain
36. pleas, please
37. pray, prey
38. pried, pride
39. pries, prise, prize
40. pros, prose
41. read, reed
42. road, rode
43. roe, row
44. roes, rows, rose
45. role, roll
46. roomer, rumor
47. rues, ruse
48. sail, sale
49. scene, seen
50. sea, see
51. seam, seem
52. sew, so, sow
53. shone, shown
54. shoot, chute
55. sighed, side
56. sighs, size
57. sign, sine
58. slay, sleigh
59. sleight, slight
60. sold, soled
61. sole, soul, Seoul
62. stake, steak
63. stayed, staid
64. steal, steel
65. stile, style
66. straight, strait
67. suite, sweet
68. swayed, suede
69. tail, tale
70. tea, tee
71. team, teem
72. teas, tease
73. throne, thrown
74. through, threw
75. tied, tide
76. toe, tow
77. towed, toad
78. vain, vane, vein
79. vale, veil
80. wait, weight
81. waste, waist
82. wave, waive
83. way, weigh
84. we've, weave

85. we, wee
86. weak, week
87. weighed, wade
88. whale, wail
89. wheel, weal
90. while, wile
91. whiled, wild
92. whined, wind

93. whole, hole
94. who's, whose
95. wreak, reek
96. wright, write, right, rite
97. wrote, rote
98. yoke, yolk
99. you, ewe, yew

CHAPTER FOUR

Odds and Ends

MISCELLANEOUS VOWEL SOUNDS

R—The control freak

Have you ever heard the term *control freak* for someone who has to dominate the situation? Well, when the letter *r* comes after a vowel, it usually exerts some power over it, changing its sound, so that we call such vowels *r-controlled*, or *r-influenced*, or *rhotic* vowels.

BRAIN TICKLERS
Set # 34

In each pair of words there are the same vowels and the letter that precedes them (if any) is the same. But in one word, the letter *r* follows the vowel(s), and in the other, there is no *r*. Compare each set of words: do they have the same vowel sounds, or different vowel sounds?

fork, fold

fur, fun

girl, give

herd, help

mirage, mileage

park, pack

tore, tone

wear, wean

work, won't

(Answers are on page 96.)

BRAIN TICKLERS
Set # 35

1. Sort the words below into groups that have the same vowel sound.

sphere	warm	four	wear
steer	worm	fir	were
dare	wore	fear	fur
welfare			

2. Add three words of your own choosing to each group you formed.

(Answers are on page 96.)

R u ready for this?

Vowel sounds influenced by the letter *r* following them are shown as wearing little hats. There are four of them: /âr/, /îr/, /ôr/, and /ûr/.

Char has the sound /âr/.
Cheer has the sound /îr/.
Chore has the sound /ôr/.
Chirp has the sound /ûr/.

Caution—Major Mistake Territory!

Other vowel sounds can appear before the letter *r* as well. You can have /ōr/, /īr/, /o͞or/ (see what follows for more about this sound), and so on. If you don't see a hat on the letter in the pronunciation, then pronounce it in the way indicated: long, short, or what have you.

BRAIN TICKLERS
Set # 36

For the sounds of /âr/, /îr/, /ôr/, and /ûr/ find as many different spellings as you can and write a word that has each spelling. You may use the chart on page 18 for help, but for every spelling you include from the chart, add a word in English (if you can find one) that uses that same spelling but isn't on the chart.

(Answers are on page 96.)

What's left?

Are we done with the vowels yet? Well, not quite. A couple of diphthongs aren't included in the long vowel category, and one other sound seems to hang out all by itself. First, the diphthongs:

/oi/ is the vowel sound in the word *boy*.

/ou/ is the vowel sound in the word *ow*.

Easy, huh?

The other sound is represented by the symbol /o͞o/, and you hear it in the word *put*.

Now try this sorting exercise.

BRAIN TICKLERS
Set # 37

1. Sort these words into groups according to the sound of the bold letters.

av**oi**d
d**ou**bt
empl**oy**
g**oo**d
H**ow**ard
p**ou**t
s**oy**
t**oo**k
w**ou**ld

2. Add three words of your own choosing to each group.

(Answers are on page 97.)

"SILENT" LETTERS

Shhhhh! Silent letter zone

Some people talk about letters that are not heard making their "usual" sound in a word as *silent*. Other people prefer to talk about these letters in other ways. Edward Carney, author of *A Survey of English Spelling*, distinguishes two kinds of *silent* letters: *auxiliary* and *dummy*.

Auxiliary letters are actually digraphs; they are combinations of letters that spell sounds that do not have a usual single letter to represent them. For example:

/*th*/ thing
/th/ there
/sh/ share
/zh/ treasure
/ng/ song

Dummy letters do not have the same kind of function that auxiliary letters do. There are two different subgroups of dummy letters. **Inert letters** are letters that appear in a word segment every time it occurs, sometimes heard, and sometimes not. For example, the *g* in
resign and *resignation*, and
malign and *malignant*
is inert.

That dummy hasn't made a sound.

You can see that the *g* is visually important in recognizing the connection between the words (that is, the word segment is the same in both cases so we know the meanings are related), even though it is pronounced in one instance and not in the other. We'll learn more about this in Chapter 7.

Empty letters are letters that seem to do absolutely nothing. They do not have a function like auxiliary letters or inert letters. The letter *u* in the word *gauge* (the only case I can find of *au* = /ā/ in English) is empty. If the word was spelled *gage*, we could read and spell it perfectly well.

Finally, final *e*

Since we are in a vowel chapter (at least so far), let's start with
the most notorious silent letter of them all—silent *e* at the end of
a word with a long vowel sound. What's it doing there, anyway?
Well, it's there as a marker to tell you that the vowel is long,
that's what. **Markers** are letters that do not represent a sound
themselves, but that tell us something about the sound of other
letters in the word. Final silent *e* is an example of a marker. It
signals a long vowel sound in the syllable it finishes. You can tell
the difference between

mat and *mate*
fat and *fate*
hat and *hate*
not and *note*
rot and *rote*
cut and *cute*
and so on,
because the *e* is marking long vowels for you.

BRAIN TICKLERS
Set # 38

Make ten sets like those above: two one-
syllable words, one of which has a short
vowel and the other of which has a final *e*
to mark the vowel as long.

(Answers are on page 97.)

A final *e* can also tell you how to pronounce *th* in words like
breath and *breathe*
cloth and *clothe*
loath and *loathe*.
And, conversely, the pronunciation—/th/ or /*th*/—can tell you
whether to spell the word with or without a final *e*.

BRAIN TICKLERS
Set # 39

Find three more pairs of words in which a
final *e* helps you know how to pronounce the
digraph *th*.

(Answers are on page 97.)

Double consonants

Well, you may point out, not all long vowels have an *e* to let you
know how to pronounce them. You're right. Another way we
recognize long vowels is that they're **not** followed by a double
consonant, a sign that often lets us know that the preceding
vowel is short. There are exceptions: *troll* with an /ō/ is one. But
many times, a double consonant at the end of a syllable means
the syllable has a short vowel sound. (There are other reasons
for doubling consonants that will be discussed later when we
talk about endings.)

BRAIN TICKLERS
Set # 40

Make a list of twenty CVCC words in which the double consonant marks the syllable as having a short vowel sound. One rule: the first letter of the two consonants that end the word CANNOT be an *r*. For example, don't use the words *hurt* or *barn,* which have *r* as the third letter.

(Answers are on page 98.)

Silent partners

We've looked at some consonants that are "silent" when they help to spell vowel sounds (at least, that's one way to interpret it). Remember these?

She's always helpful but never utters a sound.

eigh spells /ā/ in *neighbor*
is spells /ī/ in *island*
ow spells /ō/ in *mow*
hou spells /ou/ in *hour*

That's one category of silent consonants. But another category is consonants that are silent but unconnected to a vowel sound (usually in a group of two consonants). Here are some examples:

silent **b** in *comb*
silent **h** in *ghost*
silent **k** in *knight*
silent **t** in *listen*
silent **c** in *scissors*
silent **w** in *wrong*

BRAIN TICKLERS
Set # 41

1. How many words can you list that have a silent consonant letter? I have a list of 168 in the answer section (by no means a complete list). Can you find . . . 30? (NO DOUBLE LETTERS, e.g., *mm*, *bb*, and so on, ALLOWED IN THIS GAME!!) Hint: letters to focus on: *b, d, g, h, k, p, t, w*

2. Write briefly about any patterns you find.

(Answers are on page 98.)

BRAIN TICKLERS— THE ANSWERS

Set # 34, page 86

None of the sets of the words share the same vowel sound.

Set # 35, page 86

1. Possible response (it may vary depending on your dialect):
   sphere, steer, fear
   warm, wore, four
   worm, fir, fur
   dare, welfare, wear

2. Additional word possibilities:
   mere, near, gear
   door, floor, more, core
   brrr, stir, her, incur
   hair, bear, Claire, mare

Set # 36, page 88

/âr/

aer as in *aerosol*
air as in *eclair*
aire as in *solitaire*
ar as in *librarian*
are as in *hare*

ayer ODDBALL
   Can you think of
   anything besides
   prayer?
ear as in *bear*

eir ODDBALL
   Can you think of
   anything besides
   heir?
er as in *sombrero*

/îr/

ear as in *sear*
eer as in *sneer*
eir ODDBALL
   Can you think of
   anything besides
   weird?

eor ODDBALL
   Can you think of
   anything besides
   theory?
er as in *hero*
ere as in *revere*

ier ODDBALL
   Can you think of
   anything besides
   tier?

/ôr/

ar as in *warn*
aur as in *dinosaur*
oar as in *boar*

oor as in *floor*
or as in *forest*

ore as in *ignore*
our as in *pour*

/ûr/

ear ODDBALL
Can you think of anything besides *learn?*
er as in *referee*
ere ODDBALL
Can you think of anything besides *were?*
eur as in *connoisseur*

ir as in *stirrup*
irr ODDBALL
Can you think of anything besides *whirr?*
olo ODDBALL
Can you think of anything besides *colonel?*
or as in *work*

our ODDBALL
Can you think of anything besides *courtesy?*
ur as in *burp*
urr as in *purr*
yrrh ODDBALL
Can you think of anything besides *myrrh?*

Set # 37, page 89

1. avoid, employ, soy
   doubt, Howard, pout
   good, took, would

2. Additional word possibilities:
   coil, annoy, spoil
   cloud, down, proud
   book, could, foot

Set # 38, page 92

Possible responses:

Nat and Nate
hug and huge
hid and hide
rag and rage
pin and pine

kin and kine
rat and rate
pop and pope
pan and pane
glad and glade

Set # 39, page 93

Possible responses:
1. lath and lathe
2. wreath and wreathe
3. teeth and teethe
4. bath and bathe

Set # 40, page 94

Possible responses include:

back	rent	mend	dump
pack	sent	fist	rump
tack	tent	gist	bath
camp	bend	list	math
damp	lend	bump	path
lamp			

Set # 41, 95

Answers will vary, depending on your dialect.

silent *b*

bomb	debt	limb	thumb
catacomb	doubt	numb	tomb
climb	dumb	plumber	womb
comb	indebted	subtle	
crumb	lamb	succumb	

silent *c*

Connecticut	muscle	scepter	Tucson
czar	scene	science	victual
indict	scent	scissors	

silent *ch*

yacht

silent *d*

grandfather	grandpa	handsome	veldt
grandma	grandson	landscape	Wednesday
grandmother	handkerchief	sandwich	Windsor

silent *g*

align	cologne	gnarled	malign
arraign	consign	gnash	paradigm
assign	deign	gnat	phlegm
benign	design	gnaw	poignant
bologna	diaphragm	gnome	reign
campaign	ensign	gnostic	resign
champagne	feign	gnu	sign
cognac	foreign	impugn	sovereign

silent *h*

aghast	ghetto	khaki	rhubarb
annihilate	ghost	myrrh	rhyme
cheetah	ghoul	pooh	rhythm
dinghy	hallelujah	rhapsody	sorghum
exhaust	heir	rhetoric	spaghetti
exhibit	herb	rheumatism	vehement
exhort	honest	rhinoceros	
ghastly	honor	rhizome	
gherkin	hour	rhododendron	

silent *k*

knack	knell	knit	knot
knave	knickers	knob	know
knead	knife	knock	knowledge
knee	knight	knoll	knuckle

silent *l*

calf	could	palm	talk
caulk	folk	salmon	walk
chalk	half	should	would

silent *m*
mnemonic

silent *n*

autumn	condemn	hymn
column	government	solemn

silent *p*

clapboard	pneumonia	psychiatry	raspberry
corps	psalm	psychology	receipt
coup	psalter	ptarmigan	
cupboard	pseudonym	pterodactyl	
pneumatic	psoriasis	ptomaine	

silent *t*

apostle	epistle	listen	ricochet
ballet	fasten	moisten	rustle
bristle	glisten	mortgage	soften
bustle	gourmet	nestle	thistle
castle	gristle	often	trestle
chasten	hasten	pestle	wrestle
christen	hustle	potpourri	
Christmas	jostle	rapport	

silent *w*

answer	wrangle	wrestle	write
sword	wrap	wretch	writhe
two	wrath	wriggle	wrong
who	wreak	wright	wrote
whole	wreath	wring	wrought
whose	wreck	wrinkle	wrung
wraith	wren	wrist	wry

Part Two

SYLLABLE JUNCTURES

CHAPTER FIVE

Affixes: Prefixes and Suffixes

I found it!
The smallest unit
that has
meaning.

Morpheme

SYLLABLE JUNCTURES WITH PREFIXES AND SUFFIXES

Now we're going to shift our focus from vowel and consonant sounds to a more visual approach for a while. We're going to look closely at the points in words where syllables meet, known as *syllable junctures*.

Variety is the spice of syllables

The basic way we characterize syllables is by the pattern of consonant letters and vowel letters that they contain.

BRAIN TICKLERS
Set # 42

Write five words for each one-syllable word pattern.

CV	CVCe	CVVC
CVC	CVCC	CCVV
CCV	CCVC	CVCCE
CVV		

(Answers are on page 140.)

What good is a syllable juncture?

Syllable junctures (or Sjs) occur within polysyllabic words. Sometimes it's easier to spell a word if you break it into meaningful parts, and sometimes syllables are meaningful parts that you might want to use.

BRAIN TICKLERS
Set # 43

Now try combining two of the syllable patterns from Set # 42 to form polysyllabic words. How many words can you make?

(Answers are on page 140.)

BRAIN TICKLERS
Set # 44

Since many words have more than one sylla-ble, the patterns get more complex.

1. Write down ten words that have more than eight letters.

2. Find their consonant/vowel letter patterns.

3. Say the words aloud. Write down how many syllables each word has.

4. Write about any conclusions you can draw about where syllable junc-tures occur and about patterns of vowels and consonants.

(Answers are on page 140.)

Why . . . it wouldn't be the same without Syllable Juncture!

Adding affixes

When we add word parts to the beginning or end of words, we also create syllable junctures. Let me tell you about some of the vocabulary we'll be using as we explore Sjs.

base: a word element to which affixes or other bases can be added. It may be a word in itself (*logical* → *illogical*) or not (*cav* meaning "hollow" → *concave*). Sometimes these word elements—whether they can stand alone or not—are called *roots*, *root words*, or *stems*.

gender: a word's reference to whether its subject is male (like *he*) or female (like *she*). Although they are used less often today, some nouns for occupations traditionally have had both a male and female form (actor/actress; waiter/waitress).

morpheme: the molecule of word study; the smallest unit that has meaning and cannot be subdivided. It can be a base word, like *compute*; a root, like *geo*; a prefix like *anti-*; or a suffix like *-s*.

plural: the form of a noun that indicates more than one. Plurals are formed in several ways.

Singular	Plural	Change Made
pig	pigs	+s
mouse	mice	internal change
fish	fish	no change

prefix: an affix that is attached before a base.

root: see **base**.

suffix: an affix that is attached to the end of a base. A suffix can change the part of speech of the base (for example, noun to adjective: *beauty* → *beautiful*), change the tense (for example, present to past: *sniff* → *sniffed*), change the gender (*steward* → *stewardess*), or change the number (*pig* → *pigs*).

tense: the indication in a verb of whether it refers to the past, the present, or the future. There are regular and irregular verbs, which change in different ways to create tense.

	Past	Present	Present Perfect
Irregular	sang	sing	has sung
Regular	giggled	giggle	has giggled

BRAIN TICKLERS
Set # 45

Brainstorm as many occupation words that show gender as you can. If there is a form that is not gender-specific, give that also.

(Answers are on page 141.)

Double or nothing

When we change the form of a verb, or adjective, or noun by adding a suffix, this is called *inflection*. We change verbs by adding endings such as *-s*, *-es*, *-ed*, *-en*, and *-ing*, and adjectives by adding endings such as *er* and *est*.

(We'll talk about plurals in the next section.)

BRAIN TICKLERS
Set # 46

Look at each word and its inflected form. Say the words aloud. Form groups that make sense to you. What spelling patterns do you see? What general spelling rules seem to apply to the patterns you found?

big	→	bigger	rat	→	ratted
flat	→	flattest	rate	→	rating
green	→	greener	steam	→	steaming
hop	→	hopping	stem	→	stemmed
hope	→	hoping	traffic	→	trafficked
hot	→	hotter	whip	→	whipping
panic	→	panicked	wipe	→	wiped
picnic	→	picnicking	young	→	younger
radio	→	radioed			

(Answers are on page 141.)

Some of the rules you discovered may look like these:

- doubling the consonant

> Often a consonant following a short vowel is doubled before adding a suffix to signal the reader that the vowel is to be pronounced in its short form.

hop → *hopped*, not *hoped*
/hŏpt/ not /hōpt/

If the consonant is a *c* and it follows *i*, it will be "doubled" by adding *k*.

panic → *panicked*, not *panicced*

- dropping the final *e*

> Often the silent final *e* that signals a preceding long vowel is dropped before adding a suffix, because a) the reader will interpret the vowel as long without it, and b) its presence would affect the pronunciation of the suffix.

hope → *hoped*, not *hopeed*
/hōpt/ not /hō'pēd/

- changing *y* to *i*

> Often *y* is changed to *i* before a suffix, because otherwise the *y* could be read as a consonant and change the pronunciation of the suffix.

happy → *happier*, not *happyer*
/hăpēər/ not /hăp'yər/

Knowledge of how syllables fit together will help you become a better speller.

BRAIN TICKLERS
Set # 47

Use the three rules for adding suffixes: doubling consonants, dropping final *e*, and changing *y* to *i* to add the suffixes to these words.

1. bivouac + ing
2. zippy +er
3. fat +er
4. garlic + ed
5. funny + est

6. tip + ing
7. magic + ed
8. ally + ed
9. shellac + ing
10. sandy + er

11. cope + ing
12. clap + ing
13. angry + est
14. fate + ed
15. snag + ed

16. silly + er
17. slop + ed
18. havoc + ed
19. type + ing
20. slope + ed

(Answers are on page 142.)

PLURALS

Okay, we're going to take our first stab at Sjs (syllable junctures) while forming plurals of English words. This is tricky territory to navigate, because plurals are formed in different ways. Regular plurals are formed by adding -s or -es to words (*rat* → *rats* and *veto* → *vetoes*); and irregular plurals may have no change (*sheep* → *sheep*), changes in the middle of the word (*goose* → *geese*), or a host of other changes. Your best bet, if you're not sure, is to consult a dictionary.

Do-nothing plurals

This may turn out to be your favorite kind of plural. It's the kind where you look at the singular and . . . it's identical to the plural so you don't have to do a thing. Here's a list of words in which the singular equals the plural:

aircraft	humankind	samurai
alms	means	scissors
amends	moose	series
bellows	names of tribes and	shambles
chassis	races: Chinese	sheep
deer	offspring	shrimp
fish	pants (slacks)	species
forceps	proceeds	sweepstakes
goods	remains	swine
headquarters	rendezvous	United States

For American Indians/Native Americans, check with the tribe for its preferred use.

Easy street

This set of plurals follows two easy rules:

1. For most nouns in English, add -s to form the plural.

2. For nouns ending in -ch, -s, -sh, -ss, -x, or -z, form the plural by adding -es.

BRAIN TICKLERS
Set # 48

Write the plural for each of the singular nouns listed.

ax	buzz	glass
beach	church	guess
birch	crash	rush
box	dish	waltz
bus	dress	watch
bush	fox	

(Answers are on page 142.)

I say tomatoes, and you say potatoes

Most words that end in Co (consonant, *o*) add *-es* to make the plural.

dingo → *dingoes*

Words that end in Vo (vowel, *o*) add *-s* to make the plural.

stereo → *stereos*

Musical terms that come from Italian words and end in Co also add *-s* to make the plural.

alto → *altos*

Here's a list:
Consonant + *o*
echoes
vetoes
heroes
potatoes
tomatoes
lingoes
Consonant + *o*: Musical Terms from Italian
cellos
solos
pianos
sopranos
Vowel + *o*
cameos
radios
ratios
rodeos
taboos
ODDBALL
photos

Choose your own plural

Here's another category you might like. For these nouns ending in -o you can choose your own plural. Yep, believe it or not, it doesn't matter whether you add -s or -es to these words. Either way is okay!

I can't decide!

cargos or cargoes
banjos or banjoes
grottos or grottoes
hobos or hoboes
tornados or tornadoes
mosquitos or mosquitoes
volcanos or volcanoes

AND this word takes the cake with three acceptable plural forms:

buffalos or buffaloes OR buffalo—your choice.

Two different plurals—two different meanings

Some other words have two different plurals, but each plural has a different meaning. Here's a list for you to look at.

Singular	Plural # 1 and Meaning	Plural # 2 and Meaning
brother	brothers (two boys born to the same parents)	brethren (members of the same society, e.g., the Quakers)
die	dies (tools used to stamp)	dice (numbered cubes used for games)
genius	geniuses (brilliant people)	genii (imaginary spirits, like the one in Aladdin)
index	indexes (lists of book contents)	indices (algebraic signs)
staff	staves (poles or supports; the five-line systems on which music is written)	staffs (groups of assistants)

What's the difference between a dwarf and an elf?

The difference is that you form the plural of *dwarf* by adding *-s* (*dwarfs*) and the plural of *elf* by changing *f* to *v* and adding *-es* (*elves*). Here's the rule:

+ s   —f + v + es

All words ending in *f(e)* (that means either final *f* like *dwarf* or *fe* like *café*) add *s* to make the plural with the following exceptions, which change *f* → *v* and add *-es* (or if they end in *e* already, just add *-s*):

Exceptions

calf	calves	self	selves
elf	elves	sheaf	sheaves
half	halves	shelf	shelves
knife	knives	thief	thieves
leaf	leaves	wife	wives
life	lives	wolf	wolves
loaf	loaves		

The three ODDBALLS in this group are *wharf*, *scarf*, and *hoof*. For these three words, you can add either *-s* or change *f* to *v* and add *-es*, whichever you like. And, just for the record, words ending in a double *ff* (except *staff*, which has two plurals—see page 118—and *dandruff*, which isn't clearly singular or plural and has no plural form) all take the *-s* ending. For example:

sheriffs
tariffs
mastiffs

How wise are you . . .

. . . when it comes to making plural forms for nouns ending in -*y*? Here are the rules:

If the noun ends in V*y* (vowel, *y*) add -*s*.

decoy → decoys

If the noun ends in C*y* (consonant, *y*) or a consonant sound and *y* (for example, in *colloquy*, in which the *qu* sounds like /kw/), change -*y* to -*i* and add -*es*.

bunny → bunnies

BRAIN TICKLERS
Set # 49

Write the plural for each noun listed below.

beauty	donkey	soliloquy
bunny	french fry	Sunday
buy	guy	tray
city	monkey	turkey

(Answers are on page 143.)

Why can't the Romans learn to pluralize?

Foreign words can have unusual plurals, because although there may be a "regular" plural formed with -s or -es, the preferred plural is from their original language. This chart will give you an idea of some of the Latin words in this group.

Singular	Rules	Plural
alumnus cactus fungus nucleus radius	(us → i)	alumni cacti fungi nuclei radii
analysis basis crisis diagnosis hypothesis	(is → es)	analyses bases crises diagnoses hypotheses
bacterium datum medium ovum	(um → a)	bacteria data media ova
alumna antenna (insect feelers) larva vertebra	(a → ae)	alumnae antennae larvae vertebrae
matrix	(ix → ices)	matrices
criterion	(on → a)	criteria

BRAIN TICKLERS
Set # 50

Use the patterns in the foreign plurals chart to form the plurals of the following words:

antithesis	oasis	referendum
dictum	optimum	serum
focus	parenthesis	streptococcus
gladiolus	phenomenon	ulna
memorandum		

(Answers are on page 143.)

Major renovations: inside-out plurals

These are the words that change in the middle, rather than at the end.

Singular	Plural
child	children
foot	feet
goose	geese
tooth	teeth
louse	lice
mouse	mice
man	men
woman	women
ox	oxen
person	people

Which word takes the *s*?: plurals of compound words

Simple—usually you just pick the main noun and form its plural as you would if it stood alone. So:

attorney-at-law → attorneys-at-law

bachelor's degree → bachelor's degrees

man-of-war → men-of-war

mother-in-law → mothers-in-law

passer-by → passers-by

runner-up → runners-up

step-child → step-children

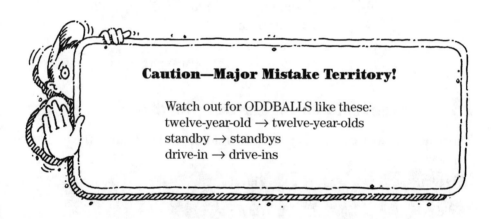

Caution—Major Mistake Territory!

Watch out for ODDBALLS like these:

twelve-year-old → twelve-year-olds

standby → standbys

drive-in → drive-ins

Plurals of proper names: Podhaizers, Yendrzeskis, Nguyens, and Dinwiddies

This is so simple that some people think it's complicated. Here's the rule:

> If the proper noun ends in *ch, s, sh, ss, x,* or *z* in the singular, add *-es*. Otherwise, just add *-s,* even if the word ends in Cy (consonant, *y*).

Singular	Plural
Adonis	Adonises
Denny	Dennys
Szymkowicz	Szymkowiczes
Choothamkhajorn	Choothamkhajorns
Lichty-Marcoux	Lichty-Marcouxes

Plurals of letters, dates, numbers, signs, and abbreviations

Easy . . . for letters, dates, numbers, and signs, just stick on an apostrophe and -s, like this:

Singular	Plural
x	x's
1990 (the year)	1990's
&	&'s
3	3's

For an abbreviation with periods, add an apostrophe and -s. If it has no periods, just add -s:

YMCA → YMCAs

Ph.D. → Ph.D.'s

Co. → → Co.'s

For more about abbreviations, see page 160.

Caution—Major Mistake Territory!

Measurement abbreviations are the same for both singular and plural.

ft, cm, tbs, in, doz

SIMPLE PREFIXES

Philosopher Gregory Bateson once—in stating the fundamental principles of education—said, "The Division of the Perceived Universe into
Parts and Whole is Convenient and May Be Necessary, . . . But No Neces-
sity Determines How It Shall Be Done." Sometimes textbooks do a dis-
service by slicing things only one way. Looking at the same object of
study from multiple perspectives may give you a greater understanding.
We're going to call this:

Slicing and dicing

We can talk about prefixes in a number of different ways.

If we talk about their:	we can gain insight into:
etymological source	the words they would likely be combined with: generally words from the same language
part of speech	the kind of word they will be attached to: generally words acting as specific parts of speech
meaning	how to use them

So we could talk about Greek prefixes (etymology); prefixes that are
prepositional, adjectival, and adverbial (part of speech); or the prefixes
micro- and *mini-*, which both mean small (meaning). Or we could just
list them all alphabetically.

BRAIN TICKLERS
Set # 51

Study this list of 47 prefixes (we'll deal with a special group called "assimilated prefixes" later). Group them in a way that makes sense to you, such as using one of the categories on the left side of the previous chart. You may find a dictionary helpful for this. Write a sentence or two about how you organized the prefixes.

Hint: When anti- precedes a base word starting with a vowel letter, you usually add a hyphen, as in *anti-American*. But for the word *antacid*, you drop the *i*. Another oddball is *cata-* in the word *category*— it loses its final *a*.

a-	without, not
a-	on, in
a-	up, out, away
amphi-	around, both
anti-	against, opposite
auto-	self
be-	around, about, away, thoroughly
bi-	two, twice
cata-	down, away, against
circum-	around, on all sides
contra-	against
counter-	opposite
de-	reversal, removal, away, from, off, down
dia-	through, together
equi-	equal
eu-	good, pleasant
extra-	beyond, outside
hemi-	half
hyper-	extra, over, excessive, beyond

hypo-	under, beneath, below
inter-	among, between
intra-	within
macro-	large
mal-	bad, wrongful
micro-	very small
mis-	wrongly, badly, not correct
multi-	many
neo-	new
non-	against, not, without
out-	to a greater degree, located externally or outside
over-	over, excessively
para-	beside, similar to, beyond
peri-	about, around
post-	after, following
pre-	before
pro-	forward, in place of, favoring
pseudo-	false, pretended, not real
re-	again, back, backward
retro-	back, backward
semi-	half, twice
super-	above, extra, over
trans-	across, beyond
tri-	three, every third
ultra-	beyond, excessively
un-	not, opposing
under-	below, beneath
uni-	one

(Answers are on page 143.)

BRAIN TICKLERS
Set # 52

1. Think of at least two words that have each prefix on the list. Some will be easy, other more complicated. Keep a list.

2. Which word or word part can you find tha works with the greatest number of these prefixes?

(Answers are on page 14

BRAIN TICKLERS
Set # 53

Using the words you've collected in Set # 5: make up a list of spelling rules that would he you in the future. Give example words to demonstrate each rule.

(Answers are on page 14

SIMPLE SUFFIXES

America's most wanted

What suffix do you think is most used? I haven't found any statistics about this, but if *-ed* isn't the most frequently used suffix, it's certainly up there. Let's take a look at *-ed* and its sound.

BRAIN TICKLERS
Set # 54

Write the past tense for each verb listed. What visual patterns do you notice?

bat	fight	pot
bide	grade	press
boil	graze	rat
catch	greet	rest
dare	hop	sail
deal	kneel	sleep
dial	lace	slop
fix	lend	snag
flap	lie	track

(Answers are on page 148.)

BRAIN TICKLERS
Set # 55

For each word in Set # 54, see if you can find a rhyme word that forms its past tense in the same way. Then, if you can, write another rhyme word that forms its past tense in a different way. Write a sentence or two about your findings.

(Answers are on page 149.)

BRAIN TICKLERS
Set # 56

Review your answers to Set # 54, this time searching for sound patterns. Use the sound patterns you find in the endings to group the words.

(Answers are on page 149.)

BRAIN TICKLERS
Set # 57

Three different things can happen to the end of a base or root when an -ed or -ing ending is added. Add both suffixes to each word below, and sort the results into three groups depending on how you treated the base word.

bump fit grate hop hope laugh rain
rub tickle

(Answers are on page 150.)

Suffix survey

Slicing, dicing, mincing, chopping, and blending

We could talk about suffixes in even more different ways than we had for prefixes.

If we talk about their:	we can gain insight into:
etymological source	the base words they would likely be combined with (generally words from the same language)
forms	how to attach them to the base word or word part they go with
meaning	how to use them
function	the effect they have on the base word they are attached to (e.g., turning a verb into a noun)

So we could talk about Latin suffixes (etymology); the suffix /ə/ and its various spellings (forms); suffixes that mean where a person is from, like *-er* and *-ian* (meaning); or the suffix *-tion* that can turn the verb *civilize* into the noun *civilization* (function). Or we could just list them all alphabetically.

Let's start with the **function** of making an adverb. Besides past tense suffixes and plurals, the adverbial suffix *-ly* is probably one of the most common suffixes. Some things adverbs with *-ly* endings can do are tell how (helplessly), to what extent (frequently), how much (slightly), and when (weekly).

This is how you add the endings to adjectives or nouns to make adverbs:

Word Ending	Change to Make Adverb	Sample
y	change *y* to *i* and add *-ly*	clumsy → clumsily
e	drop *e* and add *-ly*	gentle → gently
ll	drop one *l* and add *-ly*	dull → dully

Suf-fixation

Now let's talk about the **function** of making a noun. How many suffixes do you think there are that indicate nouns? There are at least ninety! Ninety is too many to discuss at once, so let's narrow it down to some subcategories.

BRAIN TICKLERS
Set # 58

1. For each name of a PLACE listed below, add a suffix to form the noun that names a person who comes from that place. Use this model:

   A person who comes from America is an

   _____.

   Be careful, because not all of these nouns are formed with the same suffix.

(Use a dictionary if necessary.) Make a list of the different suffixes you used.

Nigeria   Iraq   Hungary   Panama   Vermont   Japan

2. When you add a suffix to make most nouns, as in all the cases we've discussed, there are four possibilities:
   • no change
   • double the final consonant and add the suffix
   • drop the final *e* and add the suffix
   • change *y* to *i* and add the suffix

But with place names, there can be different kinds of changes. Look at these groups of nouns that indicate a place with which a person is associated. What was done to the name of each place before the suffix was added?

Swedish Finnish Polish Turkish English Irish Spanish
Canadian Peruvian Chilean Mexican Italian Jordanian
Chinese Balinese Javanese Vietnamese Taiwanese
Bengali Israeli Kuwaiti Saudi

(Answers are on page 150.)

BRAIN TICKLERS
Set # 59

Here are some suffixes that form words that tell what PEOPLE do, activities they are involved in, their vocations, or their hobbies. For each suffix, write at least one word that has that suffix. What changes did you make as you added the suffixes?

-aire	-eer	-ian
-ant	-ent	-ist
-ee	-er	-or

(Answers are on page 151.)

BRAIN TICKLERS
Set # 60

The noun suffixes listed below have to do with ideas, characteristics, attitudes, beliefs, and feelings—all ABSTRACT concepts. Read the definition and the sample word for each suffix.

1. What changes occurred in the base words as the suffixes were added?

2. Put the red words into the puzzle.

-ation state, condition, or quality of

isolate → isolation

-cy a quality or condition

dependence → dependency

-dom the condition of being ___

free → freedom

-hood state, condition, or quality of being

brother → brotherhood

-ics the science or art of

ethos → ethics

-ism a doctrine or system or principle

Buddha → Buddhism

-ment action or state

judge → judgment

-ness state, quality, or condition of being

kind → kindness

-red the condition of

hate → hatred

-ship quality or condition of

friend → friendship

-tude a condition or state of being

gratis → gratitude

-ty, ity a condition or quality

animus → animosity

(Answers are on page 151.)

BRAIN TICKLERS—
THE ANSWERS

Set # 42, page 106

Answers will vary. Possible responses:
CV: my, he, no, go, we
CVC: pig, hog, pen, cob, mud
CCV: sty, she, cry, two, gnu
CVV: May, hue, lie, boo, key
CVCe: hope, pure, love, give, vale
CVCC: sign, mold, park, warm, Turk
CCVC: know, stem, Kris, shut, Fred
CVVC: jail, boat, been, pour, boil
CCVV: free, blue, thou, flea, whoa
CVCCE: purse, horse, tense, range, bathe

Set # 43, page 106

Answers will vary. Possible responses:
CV CV	mama
CVC CVC	market
CVC CVV	coffee
CV CVVC	reboot
CVV CVV	mayday
CVV CVC	Dayton
CVC CV	manly
and so on	

Set # 44, page 107

Possible responses:
1, 2, and 3:
unanimous: VCVCVCVVC; 4 syllables
imagination: VCVCVCVCVVC; 5 syllables
understanding: VCCVCCCVCCVCC; 4 syllables
calliopes: CVCCVVCVC; 4 syllables
innovation: VCCVCVCVVC; 4 syllables
independent: VCCVCVCCVCC; 4 syllables
cauliflower: CVVCVCCVCVC; 4 syllables
melancholy: CVCVCCCVCV; 4 syllables
farsighted: CVCCVCCCVC; 3 syllables
optimistic: VCCVCVCCVC; 4 syllables

4. Answers will vary. Observations on words shown: Vowels tend to appear singly (34 times), but occasionally can be found in groups of two (4 times), whereas consonants come in groups of two (12 times) and groups of three (3 times) and also appear singly (27 times).

Often the sound of the word splits between the double or within the triple consonants. Syllables with short vowels seem to often both begin and end with consonants. Syllables with long vowels seem to end with the vowel.

Set # 45, page 110

Possible responses:

Male Form	Female Form	Non-Specific Form
businessman	businesswoman	business person
chairman	chairwoman	chair
cowboy	cowgirl	cowhand
farmer	farmerette	farmer
fireman		fire fighter
garbage man		sanitation worker
mailman; postman		mail carrier; postal worker
shepherd	shepherdess	shepherd
steward	stewardess	flight attendant
usher	usherette	usher

Set # 46, page 111

1. If you are adding -ed or -ing to a word ending in -ic, double the consonant by adding a k.

panic   panicked
picnic   picnicking
traffic   trafficked

2. If you are adding an ending to a word with a short vowel followed by a single consonant, double that consonant.

hop	hopping	big	bigger
rat	ratted	flat	flattest
stem	stemmed	hot	hotter
whip	whipping		

3. If you are adding an ending to a word with a short vowel already followed by two consonants, simply add the ending.

young younger

4. If you are adding an ending to a word with a long vowel, simply add the ending, or if the word ends in silent -*e*, drop the *e* and add the ending.

hope	hoping	steam	steaming
radio	radioed	wipe	wiped
rate	rating	green	greener

Set # 47, page 113

1. bivouacking
2. zippier
3. fatter
4. garlicked
5. funniest
6. tipping
7. magicked

8. allied
9. shellacking
10. sandier
11. coping
12. clapping
13. angriest
14. fated

15. snagged
16. sillier
17. slopped
18. havocked
19. typing
20. sloped

Set # 48, page 115

axes
beaches
birches
boxes
buses
bushes

buzzes
churches
crashes
dishes
dresses
foxes

glasses
guesses
rushes
waltzes
watches

Set # 49, page 121

beauties	donkeys	soliloquies
bunnies	french fries	Sundays
buys	guys	trays
cities	monkeys	turkeys

Set # 50, page 123

antitheses	oases	referenda
dicta	optima	sera
foci	parentheses	streptococci
gladioli	phenomena	ulnae
memoranda		

Set # 51, page 128

Possible response: I grouped the prefixes by language of origin:

Old English

a- on, in

a- up, out, away

be- around, about, away, thoroughly

mis- wrongly, badly, not correct

out- to a greater degree, located externally or outside

over- over, excessively

un- not, opposing

Greek

a- without, not

amphi- around, both

anti- against, opposite

auto- self

bi- two, twice

cata- down, away, against

dia- through, together

eu- good, pleasant

hemi- half

hyper- extra, over, excessive, beyond

hypo- under, beneath, below

macro- large

micro- very small

neo- new

para- beside, similar to, beyond

peri- about, around

pseudo- false, pretended, not real

Latin

circum- around, on all sides
contra- against
counter- opposite
de- reversal, removal, away, from, off, down
equi- equal
extra- beyond, outside
inter- among, between
intra- within
mal- bad, wrongful
multi- many
non- against, not, without
post- after, following

pre- before
pro- forward, in place of, favoring
re- again, back, backward
retro- back, backward
semi- half, twice
super- above, extra, over
trans- across, beyond
tri- three, every third
ultra- beyond, excessively
under- below, beneath
uni- one

Set # 52, page 130

1. Possible responses:

Old English

Prefix	Meaning	Examples
a-	on, in	abed, aboard, afoot, asleep
a-	up, out, away	arise, awake
be-	around, about, away, thoroughly	behead, beloved, beset
mis-	wrongly, badly, not correct	misapply, misinterpret, mismanage, misspell, mistake
out-	to a greater degree, located externally or outside	outboard, outdo, outhouse, outlive, outshine, outshoot
over-	over, excessively	overcompensate, overdrive, overdue, overrun, oversee
un-	not, opposing	unaccompanied, undo, unhappy, unlock, untrue

Greek

Prefix	Meaning	Examples
a-	without, not	amoral, apolitical
amphi-	around, both	amphibious amphitheater
anti-	against, opposite	antibody, antiseptic, antipathy
auto-	self	autobiography, automobile
bi-	two, twice	bicycle, bimonthly
cata-	down, away, against	cataclysm, catastrophe
dia-	through, together	dialogue, diameter
eu-	good, pleasant	eulogy, euphemism
hemi-	half	hemiplegic, hemisphere
hyper-	extra, over, excessive, beyond	hypercritical, hypertension, hyperthermia
hypo-	under, beneath, below	hypocritical, hypodermic, hypothesis
macro-	large	macrobiotic, macrocosm
micro-	very small	microcosm, micromanage, microscope
neo-	new	neolithic, neologism, neonatal, neo-Nazi
para-	beside, similar to, beyond	paragraph, paranormal, paraphrase, paraprofessional
peri-	about, around	perimeter, periscope
pseudo-	false, pretended, not real	pseudonym, pseudopod, pseudoscience

Latin

Prefix	Meaning	Examples
circum-	around, on all sides	circumference, circumnavigate
contra-	against	contradict, contraindicated
counter-	opposite	counteract, counterrevolution
de-	reversal, removal, away, from, off, down	deactivate, decapitate, decode, decrease, delouse, demean, destroy
equi-	equal	equidistant, equilateral, equivalent
extra-	beyond, outside	extracurricular, extraordinary, extraterrestrial
inter-	among, between	intermurals, international, interplanetary, interstate
intra-	within	intramurals, intramuscular, intravenous
mal-	bad, wrongful	malalignment, malignant, malodorous, maltreatment
multi-	many	multicolored, multiform, multimillionaire, multinational
non-	against, not, without	nonentity, nonessential, nonexistent, nonsense, nonstop, nonviolence
post-	after, following	postdate, postgraduate, postpone, postscript

Prefix	Meaning	Examples
pre-	before	preclude, prefix, preheat, prejudge
pro-	forward, in place of, favoring	proclaim, prolong, pronoun, prorevolution
re-	again, back, backward	reappear, relinquish, repair, repay, replace
retro-	back, backward	retroactive, retrorocket, retrospect
semi-	half, twice	semiannual, semicircular, semidetached, semiformal
super-	above, extra, over	supernatural, supersaturated, superscript, superstar
trans-	across, beyond	transcontinental, transpolar, transport
tri-	three, every third	triangle, tricycle, trimonthly
ultra-	beyond, excessively	ultraconservative, ultramodern, ultrasonic, ultraviolet
under-	below, beneath	underground, underhanded, underwater, underwear
uni-	one	unicycle, unison

2. Possible responses:
    active: counteractive, hyperactive, interactive, overactive, proactive, reactive, retroactive, semiactive
    do: outdo, overdo, undo
    cycle: bicycle, tricycle, recycle, unicycle
    critical: diacritical, hypercritical, uncritical
    form: deform, malform, microform, reform, uniform
    logue: catalogue, dialogue, prologue
    monthly: bimonthly, trimonthly, semimonthly
    vert: controvert, extrovert (or extravert), revert
    verse: converse, reverse, transverse, universe
    scribe: circumscribe, describe, proscribe, transcribe
    script: postscript, prescript, superscript, transcript,
    spect: circumspect, prospect, respect, retrospect

Set # 53, page 130

Possible response:

1. When adding a prefix to a base that begins with the same letter the prefix ends with, you will have a double letter: *misspell, overrun, counterrevolution*

2. When adding a prefix that ends in a vowel letter to a base that begins with a vowel letter, you will have a double vowel letter: *contraindicated, deactivate, extraordinary, reappear, retroactive, semiannual, triangle*

3. When adding a prefix to a base that begins with a capital letter, use a hyphen and keep the capital letter capitalized: *anti-American, neo-Nazi*

4. In almost every case, the prefix is spelled exactly the same way, no matter what base it is added to: *deactivate, decapitate, decode, decrease, delouse, demand, destroy*, and so on.

Set # 54, page 132

End in -ed

arrested	flapped	potted
batted	graded	pressed
boiled	grazed	ratted
dared	greeted	sailed
dialed	hopped	slopped
divided	laced	snagged
fixed	lied	tracked

End in -*t*

caught	fought	lent
dealt	knelt	slept

Set # 55, page 132

End in -*ed*

Past Tense of List Word	Past Tense of Rhyme Word	Past Tense of List Word	Past Tense of Rhyme Word	Past Tense of List Word	Past Tense of Rhyme Word
rested	ratted	flapped	trapped	potted	dotted
batted	sided	graded	faded	pressed	dressed
bided	toiled	grazed	hazed	ratted	batted
boiled	scared	greeted	heated	nested	mailed
dared	mailed	hopped	popped	sailed	cropped
dialed	nixed	laced	faced	slopped	dragged
fixed		lied	died	snagged	backed
				tracked	

End in -*t*

List Word	Past Tense of List Word	Rhyme Word	Past Tense of Rhyme Word (same)	Rhyme Word	Past Tense of Rhyme Word (different)
catch	caught			match	matched
deal	dealt			heal/steal	healed/stole
fight	fought			light	lighted/lit
kneel	knelt	feel	felt	peel	peeled
lend	lent	bend/send	bent/sent	tend	tended
sleep	slept	creep/keep	crept/kept	peep/seep	peeped/seeped

Set # 56, page 133

Past tenses ending in -*ed* with the sound /t/:

fixed	laced	slopped
flapped	pressed	tracked
hopped		

Past tenses ending in -*ed* with the sounds /id/:

graded	greeted	ratted
potted	batted	divided
arrested		

Past tenses that end in -*ed* and have the sound /d/:

boiled	grazed	sailed
dared	lied	snagged
dialed		

Past tenses ending in -*t* that end with the sound /t/:

bent	fought	lent
caught	kept	slept
dealt	knelt	

Set # 57, page 133

no change	**double final consonant**	**drop final *e***
bumped, bumping	fitted, fitting	grated, grating
laughed, laughing	hopped, hopping	hoped, hoping
rained, raining	rubbed, rubbing	tickled, tickling

Set # 58, page 136

1. Nigerian   Iraqi   Hungarian   Panamanian   Vermonter   Japanese
     -*n*   -*i*   *y* to *i*+*an*   -*nian*   -*er*   -*ese*

2. Sweden → Swedish   Finland → Finnish   Poland → Polish
   Turkey → Turkish   England → English   Ireland → Irish
   Spain → Spanish

   Canada → Canadian   Peru → Peruvian   Chile → Chilean
   Mexico → Mexican   Italy → Italian   Jordan → Jordanian

   China → Chinese   Bali → Balinese   Java → Javanese
   Vietnam → Vietnamese Taiwan → Taiwanese

   Bengal → Bengali   Kuwait → Kuwaiti   Saudi → Saudi
   Israel → Israeli

None of these groups can be explained by a single rule. The first two are very complicated groups.

Set # 59, page 137

Possible responses:

Suffix	Words that Include the Suffix		
-aire*	commissionaire	legionnaire	millionaire
-ant	debutant	assistant	descendant
-ee	referee	employee	appointee
-eer	engineer	auctioneer	rocketeer
-ent	student	correspondent	superintendent
-er	farmer	reporter	dancer
-ian	physician	musician	phonetician
-ist	typist	novelist	pianist
-or	actor	aviator	investigator

"*These words come from French . . ."

Set # 60, page 138

drop the e: isolate; dependence; judge; hate
no change: free; brother; kind; friend
drop the -os: ethos
drop the -a: Buddhism
drop the -s: gratis
drop the -us: animus

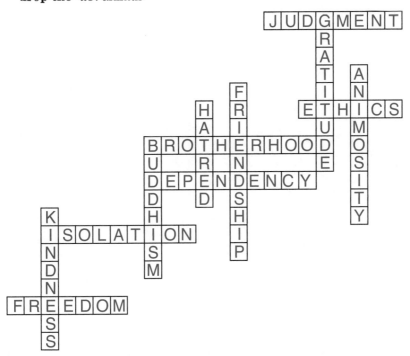

CHAPTER SIX

Compound Words and Shortened Words

COMPOUND INTEREST

Compound words are words made up of two or more whole words, not just word parts or elements. In this way, compound words are different from words with one or more affixes attached. *Antidisestablishmentarianism* is a long, sophisticated word, but it's not a compound word. It's a word with two prefixes, a base word, and four suffixes:

Prefixes	**Base**	**Suffixes**
Anti- dis-	*establish*	*-ment -arian (-ary + -an) -ism*

Deposits

Compound Interest on BASE WORDS only

Sorry NO Prefixes or Suffixes

BRAIN TICKLERS
Set # 61

Group the following compound words in categories that make sense to you. Write a sentence or two explaining your categories.

best seller
bridegroom
bull's-eye
cross-country skiing
emerald green
great-great-uncle
how-to book
ice cream

one-half mile
problem solving
stick-in-the-mud
toothache
vice-president
whiteout
whole-wheat bread

(Answers are on page 165.)

Biography of a compound

We generally distinguish three categories of compound words: **open** (in which there is space between the words); **hyphenated** (in which they are connected by a hyphen); and **closed** (in which the words are run together). In general, compounds begin their life together just sitting next to each other in sentences. This casual association happens so often that people recognize it and make the relationship of the words more formal by putting a hyphen between them. As the relationship continues, the words are thought of in such close connection that they become joined forever.

It is my personal opinion that some compound words stay in the hyphen stage and never become closed simply because they would be too difficult to read closed up.

Jack-in-the-pulpit

Does that look right to you?

Jack-in-the-pulpit (a woodland plant) is a lot easier to read at a glance than *Jackinthepulpit*. Even its shorter name, *Indian turnip*, looks pretty funny stuck together: *Indianturnip*.

To hyphenate or not to hyphenate: that is the question

Some words that exist as compounds with a particular meaning can also appear together but not as a compound and with a very different meaning. In these cases, how you connect the words can give your sentence two VERY different interpretations. My favorite example is from *Words Into Type*, page 227. Compare these two sentences:

> She used a camel's-hair brush.
> She used a camel's hairbrush.

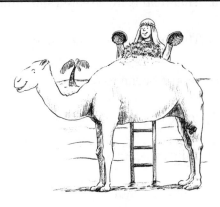

Which would you rather use on your hair?

Sometimes capital letters can help distinguish a compound word.

He lives in the white house.

is way different from

He lives in the White House.

BRAIN TICKLERS
Set # 62

Draw a picture for each sentence.

1. Wow! What a hot house!

2. Wow! What a hothouse!

3. That man is my great-grandfather.

4. That man is my great grandfather.

5. The house full of people began to dance.

6. The houseful of people began to dance.

7. She is an ancient Chinese scholar.

8. She is an Ancient Chinese scholar.

(Answers are on page 166.)

You can count on it

Because compound words go through a progression, becoming more closely linked the longer they stay together, the best way to know how to spell a compound is to look in a current dictionary. Some rules for compounds, however, are always true. And some of these rules are about using hyphens with numbers.

1. Spell all compound numbers from twenty-one to ninety-nine with hyphens.
   twenty-one   *ninety-nine*

2. Spell all fractions used as adjectives with hyphens.
   two-thirds of a foot   *three-tenths* of a mile

3. Spell all compound adjectives that contain a cardinal number followed by a noun or adjective with hyphens.
   nine-foot   *one-sided*   *two-hundred-dollar*
     board   argument   keyboard

4. Spell all compound adjectives that contain an ordinal number followed by a noun with a hyphen.
   third-story room   *first-class* accommodations

BRAIN TICKLERS
Set # 63

Form as many compounds as possible by combining words from the following list:

break	full	shine
day	light	stop
fast	moon	sun

(Answers are on page 167.)

ABBREVIATIONS

English makes use of several shortened forms of words, chiefly abbreviations and contractions.

Abbreviations take two main forms. Some abbreviations begin with the first letter of the word, include a few significant letters for a total of 3 or 4, and often end with a period. These can be the first part of the word only, as in *adj.* for *adjective,* or include the final letter as well, as in *govt.* for *government.* Sometimes consonants from throughout the word are used, as in *blvd.* for *boulevard.* The idea is to shorten the form, while giving enough information that you can recognize the word without mistake.

Acronyms are abbreviations of phrases or compound words featuring the first letters of each of the words, or of all the important words. Some acronyms are written in all capital letters (*NATO* – North Atlantic Treaty Organization), and others are written all lower case (*scuba* – self-contained underwater breathing apparatus).

COMMON ABBREVIATIONS

TIME	
A.M.	Ante meridiem (12 midnight to 12 noon)
P.M.	Post meridiem (12 noon to 12 midnight)
A.D.	Anno Domini (in the year of the Lord)
B.C.	Before Christ
B.C.E.	Before the Common Era or Christian Era
C.E.	Common Era or Christian Era
sec.	second
min.	minute
h	hour
hrs.	hours

DAYS AND DATES
Days of the Week

Sunday	Sun.	Thursday	Thurs.
Monday	Mon.	Friday	Fri.
Tuesday	Tues.	Saturday	Sat.
Wednesday	Wed.		

Months of the Year

January	Jan.	July (no abbreviation)	July
February	Feb.	August	Aug.
March	Mar.	September	Sept.
April	Apr.	October	Oct.
May (no abbreviation)	May	November	Nov.
June (no abbreviation)	June	December	Dec.

STATE POSTAL ABBREVIATIONS

Alabama	AL	Canal Zone	CZ
Alaska	AK	Colorado	CO
American Samoa	AS	Connecticut	CT
Arizona	AZ	Delaware	DE
Arkansas	AR	District of Columbia	DC
California	CA	Florida	FL

(Continued on the next page.)

STATE POSTAL ABBREVIATIONS, cont.

Georgia	GA	New Mexico	NM
Guam	GU	New York	NY
Hawaii	HI	North Carolina	NC
Idaho	ID	North Dakota	ND
Illinois	IL	Ohio	OH
Indiana	IN	Oklahoma	OK
Iowa	IA	Oregon	OR
Kansas	KS	Pennsylvania	PA
Kentucky	KY	Puerto Rico	PR
Louisiana	LA	Rhode Island	RI
Maine	ME	South Carolina	SC
Maryland	MD	South Dakota	SD
Massachusetts	MA	Tennessee	TN
Michigan	MI	Texas	TX
Minnesota	MN	Utah	UT
Mississippi	MS	Vermont	VT
Missouri	MO	Virginia	VA
Montana	MT	Virgin Islands	VI
Nebraska	NE	Washington	WA
Nevada	NV	West Virginia	WV
New Hampshire	NH	Wisconsin	WI
New Jersey	NJ	Wyoming	WY

E-MAIL AND INSTANT MESSAGE

afaik	as far as i know	imo	in my opinion
asap	as soon as possible	lol	laughing out loud
btw	by the way	np	no problem
fyi	for your information	tia	thanks in advance
imho	in my humble opinion		

WRITING ABBREVIATIONS

i.e.	id est – that is	et al.	et alia – and others
e.g.	exempli gratia – for example	etc.	et cetera – and so on

Notice that some abbreviations use periods and some don't. When in doubt, consult a dictionary.

CONTRACTIONS

Contractions, the other main kind of shortened word, are two words combined, but with several letters omitted (usually one or two). The missing letters are always indicated by the presence of an apostrophe '.

Most contractions are formed from combining a pronoun and a verb, a verb and a negative word, a question word and a verb, or a demonstrative pronoun and a form of the verb *to be*.

COMMON CONTRACTIONS

Pronoun + Verb			
I'm	I am	she'd	she had, she would
I'll	I will	it's	it is
I've	I have	it'll	it will
I'd	I had, I would, I should	it'd	it had, it would

(Continued on the next page.)

Pronoun + Verb, cont.

you're	you are (singular and plural)	we're	we are
you'll	you will	we'll	we will
you've	you have	we've	we have
you'd	you had, you would	we'd	we had, we would, we should
he's	he is, he has	they're	they are
he'll	he will	they'll	they will
he'd	he had, he would	they've	they have
she's	she is, she has	they'd	they had, they would
she'll	she will		

Verb + Negative

doesn't	does not	wouldn't	would not
don't	do not	can't	cannot
didn't	did not	couldn't	could not
hasn't	has not	mayn't	may not
haven't	have not	mustn't	must not
hadn't	had not	needn't	need not
isn't	is not	oughtn't	ought not
aren't	are not	shan't	shall not
wasn't	was not	shouldn't	should not
weren't	were not	daren't	dare not
won't	will not		

Question Word + Verb

who's	who is	when's	when is
who'd	who would, who had	where's	where is
what's	what is	why'd	why did, why would

Demonstrative Pronoun + Verb To Be

here's	here is	there'll	there will, there shall
that's	that is	there've	there have
there's	there is		

BRAIN TICKLERS— THE ANSWERS

Set # 61, page 155

Possible response:
- best seller   emerald green   ice cream   problem solving
- bridegroom   toothache   whiteout
- bull's-eye   great-great-uncle   stick-in-the-mud vice-president
- cross-country skiing   how-to book   one-half mile whole-wheat bread

Possible response: Some of the compounds are run together, some have a space between them, some are connected by a hyphen, and some have a hyphen between two of their words and space between the other two.

Set # 62, page 158

Answers in art:

1.

2.
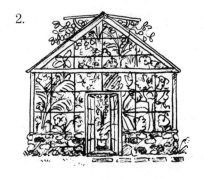

3.

4.

5.

6.

7.

8.

Set # 63, page 159

full moon
moonshine
sunshine
full stop
stoplight
sunlight
daylight
daybreak
breakfast
fast day

Part Three

DERIVATIONAL CONSISTENCY

*Derivation tells us where something comes from.
It's the same idea as etymology.
When we trace the derivation of a word,
we learn about the language in which it originated
and how it came into English. In this section we
will work toward understanding how a word's
appearance can give us clues that help us
understand meaning or sound.*

CHAPTER SEVEN

More About Suffixes

CHANGES IN SOUND

Pastry shop: what's under the crust?

Whether you prefer pie, calzone, ravioli, doughnuts, or pierogi, if you've ever bought a closed pastry you may have experienced that moment of doubt—it looks like all the others, but what's really inside? All the pastries look the same, but are they the same? There are some words like those pastries—words that look somewhat alike, but aren't pronounced alike. Fortunately, these words follow some rules of pronunciation, so they are identifiable.

They look alike but have different fillings.

Here's an example. Look at these words:

sign	signal
signed	signatory
signer	signature
signing	

All the words have the letters **s-i-g-n** in them. They look like they should all be pronounced in a similar way, but if you try saying them, you'll see that they're not. The letters stay the same to help you understand that the words have related meanings. But watch out when you spell them! Sometimes you hear the /g/ sound, and sometimes you don't, but you always have to write the letter *g*. Do you remember the term **inert letter** from Chapter 4? **Inert letters** are letters that appear in a word segment every time it occurs, sometimes heard, and sometimes not. The *g*'s that you don't hear but have to write are inert letters.

This may seem complicated or frustrating because you have to write letters that you don't hear when you say the word. But that *g* is actually useful. Here's why: Say there wasn't a *g* in the word *sign*. Then you'd spell it *s-i-n*, right? Now the complications are even greater. Is the word *sin*, /sĭn/ meaning "an offense against God" or *sin*, /sīn/ the abbreviation in trigonometry for *sine*, or sin /sēn/, as some people pronounce the twenty-first letter of the Hebrew alphabet, or is it *si[g]n* /sīn/?

You may remember that the word **morpheme** names a unit of language, like *sign*, that has a stable meaning and cannot be divided into smaller parts. It is kind of like a molecule, which is the smallest possible example of a compound.

The word *pig* is a single morpheme.

Piglet has two morphemes: *pig* and the diminutive suffix *-let*.

Pigheaded has three: *pig* and *head* and *-ed*, a suffix which makes it an adjective.

Pigheadedness has four, including *-ness*, a suffix meaning "a state or quality of being."

English tries to keep a single spelling for a single morpheme, even when the pronunciation changes. The different pronunciations of the same morphenes are called alternations.

BRAIN TICKLERS
Set # 64

For each set of words in the following list, identify the letter that is silent in one or some words and sounded in the other(s).

resign, resignation
malign, malignant
condemn, condemnation
soft, soften, softly
economical, economically /ĕk´ə-nŏm´ĭ-klē/

Reminder: The ə represents the schwa sound—the unaccented sound that is voiced like short *u*.

debt, debit
doubt, dubious
grand, grandma /grăm´ mä´/
hand, handsome, handkerchief

(Answers are on page 196.)

Everybody SH!

There are other situations in which words sound different but are obviously connected in meaning and spelling. One case is when suffixes pronounced / ən/ are added to words that end in *ic* or *t*. Once you add that ending, the *c* or *t* no longer sounds as itself, but assumes a /sh/ sound. For example, we say *connect* with a /t/ at the end, but in *connection*, we hear /sh/ and no /t/.

In British English, they change the spelling to show this: *connexion*.

The easy part for spelling is that these words just add *-ion* or *-ian* at the end, keeping their same last letter,
as in *connect* → *connection* or *physic* → *physician*.
Or, if they end in *-te*, they drop the *e* and add *-ion*.
as in *delete* → *deletion*.

BRAIN TICKLERS
Set # 65

Add an *-ion* or *-ian* ending to each word below. Underline the letter that is seen but not heard.

academic	considerate	invent
adopt	contort	logistic
assert	demonstrate	magic
associate	discriminate	music
attract	electric	pediatric
circulate	except	politic
clinic	inhibit	reflect
complete	inspect	select
composite	instruct	statistic

We'll talk more about *-ion* and *-ian* endings later.

(Answers are on page 197.)

Shorting out

In "Everybody SH!" you saw that sometimes spelling doesn't reflect the pronunciation changes that occur at the final syllable juncture when you add a suffix to a word. In the cases we looked at, there was a change in the pronunciation of the final consonant sound in the base.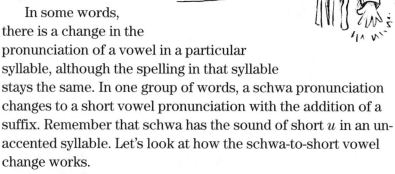

In some words, there is a change in the pronunciation of a vowel in a particular syllable, although the spelling in that syllable stays the same. In one group of words, a schwa pronunciation changes to a short vowel pronunciation with the addition of a suffix. Remember that schwa has the sound of short *u* in an unaccented syllable. Let's look at how the schwa-to-short vowel change works.

Take the words *local* and *legal*. They are each accented on the first syllable, which is pronounced with a long vowel:

Local   /lō´kəl/   Legal   /lē´gəl/

The vowel in the second syllable is a schwa. Listen to what happens when you add the ending -*ity*. The accented syllable changes to the second syllable.

Locality   /lō-kăl´ĭ-tē/   Legality   /lē-găl´ĭ-tē/

Because schwa exists only in UNaccented syllables, the sound of the second syllable CAN'T be schwa anymore, so the sound returns to the short vowel /ă/. But the spelling doesn't change.

BRAIN TICKLERS
Set # 66

Notice how you can add the suffix indicated to each base word. Underline the accented syllable in the resulting word. Identify the vowel sound you hear in that syllable.

central + -ity = centrality
economy + -ics = economics
formal + -ity = formality

metal + -ic = metallic
relative + -ity = relativity

(Answers are on page 197.)

Shorting out two

Under certain circumstances, adding a suffix can change the pronunciation of a long vowel to a short vowel—again, without a spelling change.

Take the word *please*. It has a long vowel in the accented syllable:

Please   /plēz/

Listen to what happens when you add the ending -*ant*. The accented syllable stays the same, but the long vowel becomes short:

Pleasant   /plĕz´ənt/

BRAIN TICKLERS
Set # 67

Notice how you can add the suffix indicated to each base word. Underline the accented syllable in the resulting word. Identify the vowel sound you hear in that syllable.

bile + -ious = bilious
cone + -ic = conic
crime + -inal = criminal
diabetes + -ic = diabetic

divine + -ity = divinity
mime + -ic = mimic
sane + -ity = sanity
serene + -ity = serenity

state + -ic = static
tone + -ic = tonic
volcano + -ic = volcanic

(Answers are on page 197.)

All things being equal

Do you remember that the word *schwa* comes from a Syriac word meaning "equal"—maybe because many different sounds are kind of "equalized" into one sound (more or less) in un-stressed syllables? When you add a suffix to a base word, and the accentuation of the word changes so that a syllable that was stressed is no longer stressed, a vowel with a long pronunciation can end up being pronounced as a schwa. The spelling stays the same so that you can recognize that the words are related, but the sound changes.

Take the word *compose*. It has a long vowel in the second syllable, which is accented:

Compose   /kəm-pōz´/

Listen to what happens when you add the ending *-ition*. The accented syllable changes, and the long vowel sound becomes a schwa:

Composition   /kŏm´pə-zĭsh´ən/

BRAIN TICKLERS
Set # 68

Notice how you can add the suffix indicated to each base word. Underline the accented syllable in the resulting word. Identify the change in vowel sound that occurred. What do all the base words have in common? Add two of your own, if you can.

admire + -ation = admiration
coincide + -ent = coincident
define + -ition = definition

preside + -ent = president
reside + -ent = resident

(Answers are on page 197.)

Caution—Major Mistake Territory!

None of the changes discussed in this chapter is universal—the changes described don't ALWAYS happen. You can't use them as rules for every circumstance. But knowing that they CAN happen will help you stay alert to what otherwise might be some tricky spelling circumstances.

SAME SOUND, DIFFERENT LOOK

Did you ever notice that many suffixes with identical sounds are spelled different ways? In this section we will sort out some of these homophonic suffixes so that you can understand them better.

Pay attenssion! I mean, pay attencian! Oh, just pay attention!

There are two ways of beginning to sort out the /ən/ endings in order to make sense of them: one is by sight, and the other is by sound. We will try both. To begin with, you should know that the following suffixes are in this group:

-sion   *-ssion*   *-tion*   *-cion*   *-ician*   *-en*   *-xion*

Oh, just pay atten/shən/.

BRAIN TICKLERS
Set # 69

1. First we'll focus on *-ion* words. Look at each base word.

2. Write the word made by adding the identified suffix.

3. Give the group of words a name based on how they end.

4. Tell what conclusion you can draw about how words in this grouping take an /ən/ ending.

A. All these words take the *-sion* ending:
   a. decide   evade   erode   conclude

B. All these words take the *-tion* ending
   a. compose   expose   suppose   transpose
   b. civilize   realize   specialize capitalize
   c. relax   tax   vex   fix
   d. document   indent   lament   plant

C. All these words take the *-ion* ending
   a. express   regress   possess   impress
   b. agitate   complicate concentrate educate
   c. confuse   imprecise televise   profuse
   d. constitute contribute pollute   substitute
   e. act   reflect   predict   instruct

(Answers are on page 198.)

Sound it out

Another approach to /ən/ words focuses on sound and meaning. *-ician* and *-en* are meaning groups as well as visual groups:

-ician refers to a person and his/her profession, specialty, or practice.
A *magician* is someone who is skilled in magic.
A *dietician* is a person who is professionally qualified to give guidance about diet.

-en creates a verb concerned with a meaning related to causing or becoming from an adjective:

cheap → *cheapen*   *quick* → *quicken*

OR, it forms a verb showing cause or possession from a noun:

length → *lengthen*

This leaves us with *-sion, -ssion, -tion,* and *-cion* to distinguish.

BRAIN TICKLERS
Set # 70

Try sorting these *-ion* words by sound:
/kshən/, /shən/, or /zhən/.

act	action	inspect	inspection
civilize	civilization	instruct	instruction
complicate	complication	invade	invasion
compose	composition	pollute	pollution
confuse	confusion	predict	prediction
decide	decision	profuse	profusion
expose	exposition	reflect	reflection
express	expression	regress	regression
imprecise	imprecision		

(Answers are on page 198.)

We are us, ous, ious, eous

Delicious, scrumptious, and *nutritious*! How *generous* of you to share this treat with me without *animus*. Sounds delectable, right? But how do you know when to use which spelling of /əs/? We'll try to sort out this knotty-naughty homophonic problem.

> And without animus, too!

- *-ous, ious,* and *-eous* all mean "characterized by or full of."
- *-us* is a singular Latin ending (the plural end is *-i*). It appears in words like:

Singular	Plural
alumnus	*alumni*
cactus	*cacti*
fungus	*fungi*
nucleus	*nuclei*
radius	*radii*

so its meaning puts it in a separate category from the other endings.

- Let's focus on *-ous, -ious* and *-eous* for a bit. When you attach them to a word, you can immediately hear the difference. Words like:

generous,   callous,   preposterous, and *joyous,* all with an /əs/ sound, sound different than

fallacious /shəs/, *flirtatious* /shəs/, and *courteous* /ē-əs/

- That separates out *-ous* and *-eous*. So we're left trying to tell when to use *-cious* and when to use *-tious*. *-cious* is a lot more common, so that should help, for starters. Besides that, look at the base word and see if you can make connections.

BRAIN TICKLERS
Set # 71

For each group of words, write an observation about adding *-ious* or *-eous* to it.

-atious

flirtation	flirtatious
vexation	vexatious

-acious

capacity	capacious
audacity	audacious
sagacity	sagacious
mendacity	mendacious

-nious

harmony	harmonious
ceremony	ceremonious
felony	felonious

-eous

spontaneity	spontaneous
nauseate	nauseous

-itious

nutrition	nutritious
ambition	ambitious

-icious

malice	malicious
avarice	avaricious
caprice	capricious
office	officious
suspicion	suspicious

(Answers are on page 199.)

Are you responsIBLE for choosing a suitABLE ending?

-able and *-ible* are a complicated pair.

Look at the following rules:

1. Most times that the ending is added to a whole word, you use *-able*, and when it is added to a base that cannot stand alone as a word, you add *-ible*.

Whole Word		Non-Word	
depend	dependable	aud	audible
break	breakable	ed	edible

2. If the base word ends in silent *e*
   a. preceded by a soft *c* /s/ or *g* /j/, keep the *e* and add *-able*.

   manage   manageable   notice   noticeable

   b. without a soft *c* or *g*, drop the *e* and add *-able*.

   love   lovable   use   usable

3. If the *-ion* form of the word is
   a. spelled *-ation*, add *-able.*

admire	admiration	admirable
tolerate	toleration	tolerable
transport	transportation	transportable

   b. spelled without an *a*, add *-ible*, even though it IS a whole word.

contract	contraction	contractible
produce	production	producible

   c. spelled with *ss* or *ns*, add *-ible* after the *ss* or *ns.*

permit	permission	permissible
transmit	transmission	transmissible

   There are some exceptions and additions to these rules (like *collapse*, which ends in silent *e*, but becomes *collapsible*), but these guidelines should stand you in pretty good stead.

BRAIN TICKLERS
Set # 72

Write the *-able* or *-ible* form of the following words and bases/roots:

admit	commend	read
apply	comprehend	vis-
blame	contract	
change	leg- /lej/	

(Answers are on page 200.)

Getting a hand/əl/ on /əl/

All spellings occur for a reason. But the /əl/ words have so many reasons for their different spellings that there's no simple way to categorize them. /əl/ can be spelled *el*, *le*, *al*, and occasionally *il* and *ol* (endings in *-ful* aren't included here). One important subset is *-acle*, *-icle*, and *-ical*.

BRAIN TICKLERS
Set # 73

Sometimes *el* spells the sound /əl/ at the end of a word, and sometimes it spells the sound /ĕl/. To help you remember that *el* can spell both these sounds, sort out the list of words into an /əl/ group and an /ĕl/ group.

compel	hotel	panel
excel	motel	weasel
gravel	nickel	

(Answers are on page 200.)

BRAIN TICKLERS
Set # 74

Find as many /əl/ words as you can in the word find on page 191. (There are 59.) Group them by the spelling of the /əl/ sound: *el*, *le*, *al*, *il*, *ol*, *-acle*, *-icle*, or *-ical*. Words are horizontal, vertical, or diagonal and may be forward or backward.

```
E L M P E N C I L L O E L A L O L I L A C L E E L
L E A E L C O C L I L V U L A L V E T L A C L E I
E L P E L A L I A E L W A F F L E E U O D D R A L
L E L E O M M C E R O L I L A C H E N R I U M M E
P R E T Z E L L E L O N K E M L I P N M M R R S S
L R E L U L D E D N D L L E M A C L E P P A R R F
H H E L Q R A S A N D A L A C L L E L E L E G G E
I S M M U P T T G G D L A T C L E E L E E R O C L
S E L C L E E L K E N N L I N I T I A L E A C C Z
T P P O N O L L E L D N A C N L O L L E D D U O O
O R I C M M A L R P L E L K E L E E L G N I J L O
R R I N B M B B N P P L L L E L B A F F C C U O B
I L E L A L M M E I L E L E F F B L F L E A M N M
C E L M O L Y I L R H M A C K E R E L E L L B E A
A V L L A C C A E S M A M M A L L T T L A O L L B
L I A O L R N L U S E L E G O B B L E L R R E S S
D N V B B G B B E L L A L A P B A S I L T L O Q E
D S I P E M M L S S K G G L A U B S E N N O D U L
F F T L U E Y L E I N N P L L B B V L E E D D I C
F E S B L E E S L G I E L U E L O L E L C I T R A
F E E L E S S U M N W A L O D H U L C L E L E R T
S E F L L E L T T A T L N E E D L E L E L E L E N
E S C O U N D R E L L I L O L E L A L I C L E L E
C E L A L I L O L U L A C L E I C E L C A R I M T
```

(Answers are on page 201.)

And the rooster said, "ər, ər, ər, ər, ər!"

The first thing you need to know is that some words that we spell with an -*er* suffix are spelled in British English with an -*re* suffix, and these spellings are often listed in the dictionary. Here are some examples:

U.S. Spelling	British Spelling
caliber	calibre
center	centre
fiber	fibre
liter	litre
meter	metre
saber	sabre
somber	sombre

The U.S. /ər/ words differ in the sound that precedes /ər/ and in having two different spellings: *-er* and *-ure*. (One exception is *theater/theatre*, both of which are used in the United States.)

BRAIN TICKLERS
Set # 75

Try sorting these by sound and sight. What categories do you find?

adventure	feature	picture
architecture	fracture	pleasure
closure	injure	poacher
composure	leisure	procedure
conjure	literature	sculpture
creature	measure	signature
culture	moisture	stretcher
disclosure	moocher	treasure
enclosure	overture	
exposure	pasture	

(Answers are on page 202.)

Don't let this be an instANCE for your impatiENCE

The endings *-nt*, *-nce*, and *-ncy* can all be preceded by either *e* or *a*. Some words take the ending *-ent*, and others take *-ant*. Some take *-ence*, whereas others take *-ance*. Some take *-ency*, and others take *-ancy*. Fortunately, words are consistent in taking *-e-* or *-a-* endings: *compete* takes *-ent*, and also takes *-ence* and *-ency*.

compete	competent	competence	competency

And words like *hesitate* that take *-ant*, also take *-ance* and *-ancy*.

| hesitate | hesitant | hesitance | hesitancy |

So once you know if a root word takes an *a* or an *e* in these endings, you're set. BUT . . . not every word can take all three suffixes. And sometimes the suffixes are attached to roots that cannot stand alone as words. The best thing to do is practice working with the groups.

BRAIN TICKLERS
Set # 76

For each word, give as many forms as it has for *ent/ence/ency* or *ant/ance/ancy*.

Starter	ant/ent form	ance/ence form	ancy/ency form
accept			✕
allow	✕		
annoy	✕		
buoy			
coincide			✕
confide			✕
converse			

Starter	ant/ent form	ance/ence form	ancy/ency form
correspond			
depend			
differ			✕
dominate			
emerge			
equal			
excel			
exist			✕
expect			
grief	✕		✕
hesitate			
ignore			✕
import			✕
infant	✕	✕	
magnify			✕
obey			✕
persist			
recur			✕
rely			✕
revere			✕
signify			✕
vibrate			
violate			✕

(Answers are on page 203.)

BRAIN TICKLERS
Set # 77

Some *ent/ence* words are pretty rare. For extra credit . . . over and above the call of duty . . . look up these five *ent/ence* words and note their meanings. Use the biggest dictionary you can find. (They're all in the *Oxford English Dictionary*.)

attingence   comburence   frugiferent
lutulence   regredience

(Answers are on page 204.)

BRAIN TICKLERS—
THE ANSWERS

Set # 64, page 175

g	resign, resignation
g	malign, malignant
n	condemn, condemnation
t	soft, soften, softly
a	economical, economically
b	debt, debit
b	doubt, dubious
d	grand, grandma
d	hand, handsome, handkerchief

Set # 65, page 177

academician	consideration	invention
adoption	contortion	logistician
assertion	demonstration	magician
association	discrimination	musician
attraction	electrician	pediatrician
circulation	exception	politician
clinician	inhibition	reflection
completion	inspection	selection
composition	instruction	statistician

Set # 66, page 179

cen**tral**ity	short *a*	/ă/
eco**nom**ics	short *o*	/ŏ/
for**mal**ity	short *a*	/ă/
me**tal**lic	short *a*	/ă/
rela**tiv**ity	short *i*	/ĭ/

Set # 67, page 180

bilious	short *i*	/ĭ/
conic	short *o*	/ŏ/
criminal	short *i*	/ĭ/
dia**be**tic	short *e*	/ĕ/
di**vin**ity	short *i*	/ĭ/
mimic	short *i*	/ĭ/
sanity	short *a*	/ă/
se**ren**ity	short *e*	/ĕ/
static	short *a*	/ă/
tonic	short *o*	/ŏ/
vol**can**ic	short *a*	/ă/

Set # 68, page 181

admi**ra**tion	long *i* /ī/ goes to /ə/
co**in**cident	long *i* /ī/ goes to /ə/
defi**ni**tion	long *i* /ī/ goes to /ə/
president	long *i* /ī/ goes to /ə/
resident	long *i* /ī/ goes to /ə/

Possible responses: *perspire → perspiration*   *inspire → inspiration*

Set # 69, page 183

Words ending in *de* drop the *de* and add *-sion*.

decide	decision	erode	erosion
evade	evasion	conclude	conclusion

Words ending in *ose* drop the *e* and add an *i* before *-tion*

compose	composition	suppose	supposition
expose	exposition	transpose	transposition

Words ending in *ize* drop the *e* and add an *a* before *-tion*

civilize	civilization	specialize	specialization
realize	realization	capitalize	capitalization

Words ending in *x* and *nt* add *a* before *-tion*.

relax	relaxation	document	documentation
tax	taxation	indent	indentation
vex	vexation	lament	lamentation
fix	fixation	plant	plantation

Words ending in *ss* add *-ion*.

express	expression	possess	possession
regress	regression	impress	impression

Words ending in *ate, ise, use,* and *ute* drop the *e* and add *-ion*.

agitate	agitation	televise	television
complicate	complication	profuse	profusion
concentrate	concentration	constitute	constitution
educate	education	contribute	contribution
confuse	confusion	pollute	pollution
imprecise	imprecision	substitute	substitution

Words ending in *ct* add *-ion*.

act	action	predict	prediction
reflect	reflection	instruct	instruction

These visual groups can help you predict spelling, but there are exceptions.

Set # 70, page 185

/kshən/

act	action	predict	prediction
inspect	inspection	reflect	reflection
instruct	instruction		

/shən/

civilize	civilization	express	expression
complicate	complication	pollute	pollution
compose	composition	regress	regression
expose	exposition		

/zhən/

confuse	confusion	invade	invasion
decide	decision	profuse	profusion
imprecise	imprecision		

Set # 71, page 187

Answers may vary. Possible responses:

-atious

Words that have an -*ation* form take -*atious*.

flirtation	flirtatious	vexation	vexatious

-acious

Words that have an -*acity* form take -*acious*.

capacity	capacious	sagacity	sagacious
audacity	audacious	mendacity	mendacious

-nious

Words that have an -*ony* form take -*nious*.

harmony	harmonious	felony	felonious
ceremony	ceremonious		

-eous

Words with an *e* after the last consonant in the root take *e*.

spontaneity	spontaneous	nauseate	nauseous

-itious

Words with an -*ition* form take -*itious*.

nutrition	nutritious	ambition	ambitious

-icious

Words with an -*ic(e)* take -*icious*.

malice	malicious	office	officious
avarice	avaricious	suspicion	suspicious
caprice	capricious		

Set # 72, page 189

admit	admissible	comprehend	comprehensible
apply	applicable	contract	contractible
blame	blamable	leg- /lej/	legible
change	changeable	read	readable
commend	commendable	vis-	visible

Set # 73, page 190

/ĕl/		/əl/	
compel	hotel	gravel	panel
excel	motel	nickel	weasel

Set # 74, page 190

```
E L M P E N C I L L O E L A L O L I L A C L E E L
L E A E L C O C L I L V U L A L V E T L A C L E I
E L P E L A L I A E L W A F F L E E U O D D R A L
L E L E O M M C E R O L I L A C H E N R I U M M E
P R E T Z E L L E L O N K E M L I P N M M R R S S
L R E L U L D E D N D L L E M A C L E P P A R R F
H H E L Q R A S A N D A L A C L L E L E L E G G E
I S M M U P T T G G D L A T C L E E L E E R O C L
S E L C L E E L K E N N L I N I T I A L E A C C Z
T P P O N O L L E L D N A C N L O L L E D D U O O
O R I C M M A L R P L E L K E L E E L G N I J L O
R R I N B M B B N P P L L L E L B A F F C C U O B
I L E L A L M M E I L E L E F F B L F L E A M N M
C E L M O L Y I L R H M A C K E R E L E L L B E A
A V L L A C C A E S M A M M A L L T T L A O L L B
L I A O L R N L U S E L E G O B B L E R R E S S
D N V B B G B B E L L A L A P B A S I L T L O Q E
D S I P E M M L S S K G G L A U B S E N N O D U L
F F T L U E Y L E I N N P L L B B V L E E D D I C
F E S B L E E S L G I E L U E L O L E L C I T R A
F E E L E S S U M N W A L O D H U L C L E L E R T
S E F L L E L T T A T L N E E D L E L E L E L E N
E S C O U N D R E L L I L O L E L A L I C L E L E
C E L A L I L O L U L A C L E I C E L C A R I M T
```

LE

bamboozle	fable	puddle
bubble	gobble	ripple
bumble	jingle	rumple
camel	jumble	tattle
candle	maple	tickle
curdle	marble	turtle
dimple	needle	twinkle
eagle	pretzel	waffle

ACLE

miracle	tentacle

ICLE

article	icicle	vehicle

ICAL

historical	radical

AL

central	mammal	signal
cymbal	opal	spinal
festival	oval	
initial	sandal	

EL

angel	hovel	scoundrel
bushel	kernel	snivel
camel	mackerel	squirrel
colonel	mussel	tunnel

OL

carol	idol	symbol

IL

basil	pencil	stencil

Set # 75, page 193

Two Syllables
/chər/

creature	moisture	poacher
culture	moocher	sculpture
feature	pasture	stretcher
fracture	picture	

/zhər/

closure	measure	treasure
leisure	pleasure	

/jər/

conjure	injure

Three or More Syllables
/chər/

adventure	literature	signature
architecture	overture	

/zhər/
composure   enclosure   exposure
disclosure

/jər/
procedure

Set # 76, page 194

	ant/ent form	ance/ence form	ancy/ency form
accept	acceptant	acceptance	
allow		allowance	
annoy		annoyance	
buoy	buoyant	buoyance	buoyancy
coincide	coincident	coincidence	
confide	confident	confidence	
converse	conversant	conversance	conversancy
correspond	correspondent	correspondence	correspondency
depend	dependent	dependence	dependency
differ	different	difference	
dominate	dominant	dominance	dominancy
emerge	emergent	emergence	emergency
equal	equivalent	equivalence	equivalency
excel	excellent	excellence	excellency
exist	existent	existence	
expect	expectant	expectance	expectancy
grief		grievance	
hesitate	hesitant	hesitance	hesitancy
ignore	ignorant	ignorance	
import	important	importance	
infant			infancy
magnify	magnificent	magnificence	
obey	obedient	obedience	
persist	persistent	persistence	persistency
recur	recurrent	recurrence	
rely	reliant	reliance	
revere	reverent	reverence	
signify	significant	significance	
vibrate	vibrant	vibrance	vibrancy
violate	violent	violence	

Set # 77, page 196

attingence: influence
comburence: ability to cause combustion, that is, start a fire
frugiferent: bearing fruit
lutulence: muddiness
regredience: return

CHAPTER EIGHT

Confusing Words

HOMOGRAPHS AND HOMOPHONES

Present a present and record a record

Homographs are groups of (usually two) words that are spelled the same way but have different meanings. There are several kinds of homographs.

Related verbs and nouns (like record´ and re´cord) with the same spelling but different pronunciations, are not technically homographs because they have the same etymological root, but we're going to include them here because they can present a spelling challenge—you have to remember that even though they sound different, they're spelled the same.

Other related parts of speech can be homographs AND homophones at the same time. When one, for example, has a comparative ending -er and the other has the noun suffix -er, you get homographs like:

stranger (the person you don't know) and *stranger* (more strange)

cooler (the place you keep things so they don't get warm) and *cooler* (more cool).

BRAIN TICKLERS
Set # 78

For each word in the list below, look in the dictionary to find definitions for two homographs that are NOT homophones. Record the definitions.

1. bass   3. gill   5. real

2. bow   4. lead

(Answers are on page 212.)

BRAIN TICKLERS
Set # 79

Use the clues to help you discover the homographs that will complete the crossword puzzle.

DOWN

1. Several female deer, or the third person singular of a verb meaning "to carry out"

3. Very small, or a duration of time equal to 60 seconds

4. The quality of not being dead, or a verb meaning "to reside in a place"

6. A kind of fish with both eyes on one side of its head, or to thrash about helplessly and without effect

7. Creating a small, bright sound as by hitting a crystal with a pencil, or coloring something slightly

8. Hitting a golf ball a short distance, or the act of placing something in a spot

9. Moving air, or the act of wrapping up something into a ball

ACROSS

2. To start up again, or an organized list of one's activities and employment

5. To strike with sharp blows, or a display of food from which guests may serve themselves

9. Wrapped up string into a ball, or an injury that breaks the skin

(Answers are on page 213.)

What's /sôs/ for the goose, may be /sŏs/ for the gander

Homophones are groups of (usually two) words that sound the same but are spelled differently. But different people may have different homophones. Why? Because homophones depend on pronunciation, and people with different dialects pronounce words differently. What's a homophone for you may not be a homophone for your best friend.

Hum oh funs

There are several kinds of homophones:

- Single words that come from the same origin, but evolved differently.
- Single words that have different origins.
- A single word or group of words that sounds identical to another group of words, either in English or in another language.

Homonyms

When a pair of homographs are also homophones, we call them *homonyms*. Got that? They're word pairs that are spelled the same AND pronounced the same. Examples are
cricket (the game and the insect)
can (the container and the verb that means "to be able")
fine (the penalty and the adjective meaning "good").

Caution—Major Mistake Territory!

Just because a word has more than one meaning listed in the dictionary DOESN'T mean you've found a homonym. You can tell homonyms because they are separate bold-faced entries with the same pronunciation.

BRAIN TICKLERS
Set # 80

1. Write a homophone for each word listed.

brews	freeze	pores
brows	grays	tax
daze	hose	tease
doze	nose	wax
flew		

2. How many sets of homonyms can you list in five minutes? Time yourself and see. (No fair using the homophones from #1.)

(Answers are on page 214.)

BRAIN TICKLERS—
THE ANSWERS

Set # 78, page 207

Possible responses include the following:

1. **bass:** a freshwater fish; a man with a low singing voice; a fibrous plant product

2. **bow:** the front of a ship; to bend one's body in recognition of applause; a rod strung with horsehair and used for playing a string instrument such as a violin

3. **gill:** a fish's respiratory organ; a unit of liquid measure equal to 1/2 cup

4. **lead:** to guide; a soft metal

5. **real:** actually the case; a Portuguese and Brazilian monetary unit

Set # 79, page 208

```
        D
        O
R E S U M E     L
  S     I       I
        N       V
    B U F F E T
        T   L   I
        E   O   N
            U   G
        P   N   I
  W O U N D     N
    I   T   E   G
    N   T   R
    D   I
        N
        G
```

Set # 80, page 211

1. brews/bruise   hose/hoes
   brows/browse   nose/knows/no's
   daze/days   pores/pours
   doze/doughs   tax/tacks
   flew/flue   tease/teas
   freeze/frieze/frees   wax/whacks
   grays/graze

2. Possible responses:
   bank: the earth beside a river; a monetary institution
   bark: the sound a dog makes; the covering on a tree trunk
   barrow: short for wheelbarrow; a burial mound or hill
   bellows: yells loudly; a tool for providing oxygen to a fire
   bound: tied up; headed towards
   can: a metal container; capable of
   champ: to chew; the champion
   cricket: a sport; an insect resembling a grasshopper
   fare: amount required for a bus/subway/taxi ride; food
   fine: a penalty; good
   firm: unyielding; a company
   fit: a seizure; in good shape, healthy
   flat: an apartment; a level
   hail: to greet; hard, round precipitation called "hailstones"
   hamper: to get in the way of; a container, especially for dirty laundry
   last: a shoemaker's tool; the final one
   leaves: goes away; the things that fall off trees in autumn
   mews: a back street; the noise a cat makes
   mine: a deep pit, dug to allow removal of gems and minerals from the earth; something that belongs to me
   pants: breathes heavily to reduce internal body temperature; slacks
   plane: a two-dimensional surface; a type of tree
   quarry: something that's being hunted; a place where stones are mined
   rest: a nap; what's left over
   rose: a flower; got up
   row: an argument; to use an oar or set of oars to propel a boat
   stable: steady; a place to keep horses

CHAPTER NINE

Greek and Latin Base Words

FAMILY RESEMBLANCE

In Chapter 5 we talked about prefixes with Greek and Latin origins, as well as Latin plurals. But since many important base words come to us from Greek and Latin and form the foundation of some hefty word families, we're going to take some time to focus on them. The important point from a spelling perspective is that these word families all have a family resemblance, kind of like everyone in a family having curly hair or freckles—some feature that helps you identify that they go together. For the

most part, once you know the spelling of a base, there is not a lot of variation. If you can spell *metr/meter*, the Greek root meaning "measure," you can spell it in *symmetry, diameter, metric, geometry, thermometer,* and so on. Familiarity with these widely used roots will improve your spelling.

BRAIN TICKLERS
Set # 81

Just to get you started . . . take a look at these root words and their meanings. Write as many English words as you can that have each root word. You can use a dictionary if you wish. Remember that you can have the root word appear at the beginning, middle, or end of an English word, and you can add prefixes, suffixes, or both to it.

Greek Root	Meaning	Example in English
aster/astr	star	astronaut
auto	self	automatic
chron	time	chronic
graph	writing	paragraph
Latin Root		
scrib/script	to write	scribe
son	sound	sonic
verb	word	verbal
voc/vok	to call/voice	vocal chords

(Answers are on page 230.)

Sound familiar?

It's easier to remember a group of interconnected words than just a random list of roots. So let's look at some logically connected groups of root words. First let's focus on words having to do with sound.

Sound

Root Word	Meaning	Language of Origin	Example
dic/dict	speak	Latin	dictate
phe/phem	speak	Greek	euphemism
gloss/glott/glot	tongue/language	Greek	polyglot
lingu	language/tongue	Latin	linguistic
aud	hear	Latin	audible
ora	speech/mouth	Latin	oracle
phon	sound	Greek	phonograph

BRAIN TICKLER
Set # 82

How many English words can you discover that contain at least one of the root words in the Sound chart on page 219?

(Answers are on page 231.)

Vision revision

Many English words having to do with looking, seeing, the eye, and tools used with the eye have Greek and Latin roots.

Sight

Root Word	Meaning	Language of Origin	Example
luc	light	Latin	lucid
ocul	eye	Latin	ocular
ops/opt/op	sight; eye	Greek	optical
photo/phos	light	Greek	photograph
scope	instrument for viewing	Greek	microscope
spect	look	Latin	prospect
vid/vis	to see	Latin	video

BRAIN TICKLERS
Set # 83

This time, tell the meaning of each word made from one of the roots in the sight chart.

photograph	phosphorescent
telescope	elucidate
inspect	monocle
invisible	ophthalmologist

Look up the word in a dictionary if you need to.

(Answers are on page 232.)

The law of the land

Just as our legal system and our system of government have their origins in Greece and Rome, so do many of our words having to do with right and justice (the judicial branch) and governing (the executive branch) come from these two civilizations.

Hey! Watch your step!

Right/Justice

Root Word	Meaning	Language of Origin	Example
bon/ben	good	Latin	bonus
crit/cris	judge	Greek	critical
dox	opinion	Greek	paradox
eth	moral	Greek	ethos
jud	judge	Latin	judge
mal	bad	Latin	malfunction
nom	law	Greek	Deuteronomy
ortho	correct/straight	Greek	orthopedics
ooph	wise	Greek	sophisticated
val	strong/worth	Latin	valuable

Governing

Root Word	Meaning	Language of Origin	Example
arch	rule/govern	Greek	matriarch
cracy	rule/government	Greek	autocracy
dem	people	Greek	epidemic
ethn	nation	Greek	ethnicity
pol/polis	city, state	Greek	politics

BRAIN TICKLERS
Set # 84

Read each clue and write the word containing one of the "Law of the Land" roots that fits into the crossword puzzle. Notice which spelling is used for the roots that have alternate forms.

DOWN

1. Accepting an established doctrine

4. To evaluate

5. The absence of a ruler

6. Wrongdoing by someone who holds public office

7. Not legally valid

8. Having to do with a major city

ACROSS

2. Principles of moral value

3. Having to do with courts of law

9. Working for the good of

10. Reasoning that appears wise, but isn't

11. Rule by the people

12. Relating to racial and cultural heritage

13. Rule of a single person by him/herself

(Answers are on page 232.)

To life!

Life

Root Word	Meaning	Language of Origin	Example
anim	spirit/life	Latin	animated
dendr/dender	tree	Greek	dendrology
spir	to breathe	Latin	perspire
vit/viv	life	Latin	vital
zoo	animal	Greek	zoo

While at the zoo, the dendrologist began to perspire when the vital life-form became a little too animated.

BRAIN TICKLERS
Set # 85

Put these words of Latin and Greek origin from the list below into the puzzle to make the mystery word appear in the vertical box.

animal   spirit
inspiration   vivid
rhododendron   zoology

Mystery word clue:

It originally meant "those who share a stream" and now means "competitors." Find this word that comes from a Latin root.

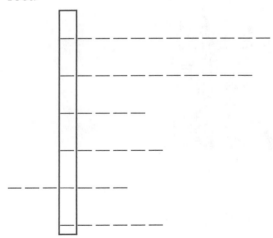

(Answers are on page 232.)

Miscellaneous but not extraneous

Here are three more categories—size, love, and study—and a challenge to go with them.

BRAIN TICKLERS
Set # 86

If you can find one word that contains each root word, you're floating; two, and you're in orbit; three or more, and you're on the astral plane.

Size

Root Word	Meaning	Language of Origin
magna	large	Latin
mega/megalo	large	Greek
micro	small	Greek

Love

Root Word	Meaning	Language of Origin
ama/ami	love	Latin
philo	love	Greek

Study

Root Word	Meaning	Language of Origin
doc/doct	teach	Latin
gno/gnos	know	Greek
logo	word/reason	Greek
sci	know	Latin
ver	truth	Latin

(Answers are on page 233.)

BRAIN TICKLERS
Set # 87

Now it's time to review what you've learned. Write a composition in which you use at least ten words, each having a different Greek or Latin root used in this chapter. You can write a short story, a news story, a diary entry, or any other kind of piece that strikes your fancy. Try to choose your topic carefully to make your work easier.

(Answers are on page 233.)

BRAIN TICKLERS
Set # 88

The final challenge . . . Can you take some of the prefixes from Chapter 5 and combine them with the roots here to make new words? Use clues to help you. Combine Greek prefixes with Greek roots and Latin prefixes with Latin roots. Use a dictionary to help you if you need to.

Greek Prefixes	Clues Make Words that Mean:
a- (*an-*) without, not	"not knowing" "without leadership"
anti- against, opposite	"against the law" "opposition"
auto- self	"rule by a single person"
dia- through, together	"to talk together"
eu- good, pleasant	"a pleasant way of speaking about an unpleasant topic"
hyper- extra, over, excessive, beyond	"overcritical"
micro- very small	"an instrument that enlarges a small sound"
para- beside, similar to, beyond	"beyond opinion"
peri- about, around	"an instrument that allows one to look around corners"
pseudo- false, pretended, not real	"with a false appearance of refinement"

Latin Prefixes	Clues Make Words that Mean:
bi- two	"having two lenses" "for both eyes"
circum- around, on all sides	"to look around" "prudent"
de- reversal, removal, away, from, off, down	"to reduce the value of"
multi- many	"able to speak many languages"
pre- before	"to evaluate before sufficient evidence is available"
re- again, back, backward	"to look at again in order to correct" "to make move again" "to make live again"
trans- across, beyond	"letting light shine through" "to breathe out"

(Answers are on page 234.)

BRAIN TICKLERS—
THE ANSWERS

Set # 81, page 218

Possible responses:

Greek	
aster/astr	asterisk asteroid astral astrocyte astrodome astrodynamics astrogate astrology astrometry astronautics astronavigation astronomer astronomical astronomy astrophotography astrophysics astrosphere disaster

auto	autobiographer autobiography autochrome autochthon autoclave autocrat autograph autoharp autohypnosis automat automobile autonomy autopsy photoautotroph semiautobiographical semiautomatic
chron	anachronism chronicle chronograph chronology chronometer dendrochronology synchronize
graph	autobiography autograph bibliography biography calligraphy grapheme graphic graphite phonograph photograph telegraph

Latin

scrib/script	ascribe circumscribe describe description inscribe inscription manuscript nondescript prescribe prescription scribble script scripture subscribe transcribe transcript
son	consonant diapason dissonance resonance sonata sonnet sonogram sonorous
verb	adverb nonverbal proverb reverb verbal verbalize verbatim verbiage verbose
voc/vok	advocate equivocate evoke invocation invoice irrevocable provoke provocateur revoke subvocalize vocabulary vocal vocalist vocation vociferous

Set # 82, page 220

aud	audience, audio, audition, auditorium, auditory, inaudible
dic/dict	benediction, contradict, contradiction, dictator, diction, dictionary, edict, indict, malediction
gloss/glott/glot	epiglottis, glottal, gloss, glossary, glossolalia, polyglot
lingu	bilingual, lingo, linguine(!), linguist
ora	oracle, oral, oration, oratorio
phe/phem	blaspheme, prophet
phon	aphonic, cacophony, euphony, megaphone, microphone, orthophonic, phonics, polyphony, symphony, telephone

Set # 83, page 221

photograph: a print made on light-sensitive paper
telescope: an instrument to see things that are far away
inspect: to look at closely
invisible: not able to be seen
phosphorescent: permitting emission of light after exposure to radiation
elucidate: to bring to light; to make plain
monocle: a single lens used to improve vision
ophthalmologist: a physician specializing in the function and diseases of
the eye

Set # 84, page 223

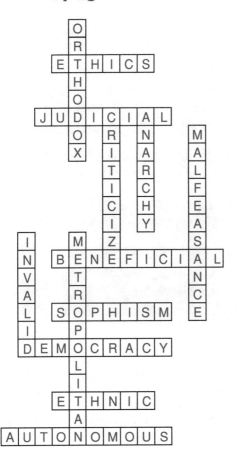

Set # 85, page 226

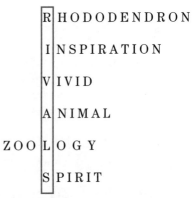

R HODODENDRON

I NSPIRATION

V IVID

A NIMAL

ZOO **L** O G Y

S PIRIT

The words spell *rivals*,
which is the mystery word.

Set # 86, page 227

Size

magna	magnanimous magnate magnification magnificent magnify magniloquent magnitude
mega/megalo	megabucks megabyte megahertz megalith megalomaniac megalopolis megaphone megavitamin
micro	microbe microbiology microchip microeconomics microelectronics micromanage microphone

Love

ama/ami	amateur amiable amicable amigo amity
philo	Anglophile bibliophile hemophilia Philadelphia philanthropy philately philodendron philology philosophy

Study

doc/doct	docile doctor doctorate doctrine docudrama documentary indoctrinate
gno/gnos	agnostic diagnosis gnosticism prognosticate
logo	analogy archaeology catalogue dialogue eulogy genealogy geology logic monologue prologue syllogism
sci	omniscient prescience science scientific scientist
ver	veracious veracity veridical verdict verification verify verisimilitude veritable verity

Set # 87, page 228

Possible response: a poem

Once there was an <u>astronaut</u>, who also was a <u>polyglot</u>.

He went on many <u>astral</u> trips in spaceships that used <u>microchips.</u>

He wasn't one to cry or mope. He <u>verified</u> sightings through the <u>telescope</u>.

One day, alas, his spaceship crashed; his fine equipment all was trashed.

He went out to <u>inspect</u> the mess, and think and probe and <u>judge</u> and guess and <u>prospect</u> for some things of worth, so he could travel back to Earth.

<u>Prognosticating</u> by the moon, he hoped that he could get back soon.

Employing <u>scientific</u> means, he built a worthy craft, it seems.

For since arriving back today, he's left to vacation in Paraguay.

But soon he'll be back out in space, exploring some new distant place.

Set # 88, page 229

Greek

"not knowing"	agnostic
"without leadership"	anarchy
"against the law" "opposition"	antinomy
"rule by a single person"	autocracy
"to talk together"	dialogue

"a pleasant way of speaking about an unpleasant topic"	euphemism
"overcritical"	hypercritical
"an instrument that enlarges a small sound"	microphone
"beyond opinion"	paradox
"an instrument that allows one to look around corners"	periscope
"with a false appearance of refinement"	pseudo-sophisticated

Latin

"having two lenses" "for both eyes"	binoculars
"to look around" "prudent"	circumspect
"to reduce the value of"	devalue
"able to speak many languages"	multilingual
"to evaluate before sufficient evidence is available"	prejudge
"to look at again in order to correct"	revision
"to make move again"	reanimate
"to make live again"	revive
"letting light shine through"	translucent
"to breathe out"	transpire

CHAPTER TEN

Predictable Spelling Changes: Changes in Sight

NOW YOU SEE IT, NOW YOU DON'T

In Chapter 7 we talked about alternations—changes in sound that occur even though spelling stayed the same. Now we're going to discuss changes in spelling that come about mainly to make words easier to pronounce. When we add affixes to roots, sometimes the result is kind of hard to say. We accommodate these situations with little shifts that help us get our tongues around the words.

Look at these suffix additions and try saying the results without and with the accommodation. Which works best, do you think?

Root + Suffix	Result without Accommodation	Pronunciation	Result with Accommodation
erode + sion	erodsion	/ĭr-ōd´shən/	erosion
comprehend + sion	comprehendsion	/kŏm-prĭ-hĕnd´shən/	comprehension
introduce + tion	introducetion	/ĭn-trə-dōōs´shən/	introduction
magic + ian	magician	/mă-jĭk´shən/	magician

WOW!

Better, right?

_e r o s i o n_

Remember this? Changes at the syllable juncture

Remember how we dealt with spelling changes needing to match sound changes when we added /ən/? Then we were differentiating /ən/ endings. Now we're going to focus on the spelling changes that happen when these suffixes are added.

D and DE changes	erode *de* spells /d/	→	erosion *s(i)* spells /zh/
	comprehend *d* spells /d/	→	comprehension *s(i)* spells /sh/
CE changes	introduce *ce* spells /s/	→	introduction *c* spells /k/
C changes	magic *c* spells /k/	→	magician *c(i)* spells /sh/

BRAIN TICKLERS
Set # 89

Write the *-ion* or *-ian* form of each word given below. Group the resulting words into the groups represented in the chart above:

$$D \to S \qquad DE \to S \qquad CE \to C \qquad C \to CI$$

collide	extend	music	produce
decide	include	persuade	reduce
delude	invade	politic	statistic
explode	mathematics		

(Answers are on page 251.)

What's happening to my vowels?

Sometimes adding a suffix changes more than just the syllable juncture. Yes, back in the middle of the word, things can change, too. Remember how adding a suffix can change pronunciation? We talked about these alternations in Chapter 7. Often, these changes were either from or to a schwa sound, and since schwa can be spelled with virtually any vowel letter, the spelling didn't change.

Now we're getting to more sophisticated changes: Sometimes the sound AND the spelling change. Remember the word *morpheme*? It's the smallest unit of language that has meaning and cannot be subdivided. However, a single morpheme can have more than one appearance or shape. When you have more than one visual/sound form of a morpheme, the multiple forms are called *allomorphs*. Here are two examples:

vain in *vain* and **van** in *vanity* are the same morpheme. When you add the suffix *-ity* the long *a* spelled *ai* becomes an *a*, and the vowel sound changes from long to short. In adding the suffix *-ity* to a word like *insane*, dropping the *e* is enough to signal the change from a long to a short vowel sound. No other spelling change is needed.

sume in *consume* and **sump** in *consumption* are also the same morpheme. When you add the suffix *-tion* the long *u* marked by the final *e* changes to a *u* followed by a double consonant, indicating a short pronunciation—again, a change from long to short. Notice that in both cases, the accented syllable remains the same.

Some allomorphs have a long version and a schwa version for when the accentuation changes syllables, and often the spelling changes as well. So we get:
explain′ → explana′tion **plain** → **plan** and the accent moves to the following syllable
exclaim′ → exclama′tion **claim** → **clam** and the accent moves to the following syllable
Notice how the initial vowel in the digraph stays the same—the vowel with which the sound is named—and the second vowel is dropped.

BRAIN TICKLER
Set # 90

Given the previous examples, predict the vowel change for each bold syllable when adding the suffix indicated. Then write the word with the suffix. Use a dictionary if you need to.

re**ceive** + tion
per**ceive** + tion
de**ceive** + tion
state + ic
tone + ic

bile + ious
grain + ular
mime + ic
flame + able

(Answers are on page 251.)

ASSIMILATION INVESTIGATION— MEET THE CHAMELEONS

And I thought I knew a thing or two about assimilation!

Now we're going to wind up our exploration of spelling with the most changeable of all morphemes: a set of prefixes that change their final consonant in order to better fit with the root or base word they attach to. Just like a chameleon that changes its color to match its surroundings, these guys change their shape to better fit in with whatever follows—to smooth out the syllable juncture, as it were. This can make them tricky to recognize, because they look one way one time, and a different way the next time—these prefixes have more allomorphs than you can shake a stick at. So let's start off by meeting them.

The basic six

Here they are:

Prefix	Meaning(s)
ad	to, toward
com	with
in	not, into
ob	against, toward
sub	under
syn	together, with

BRAIN TICKLERS
Set # 91

Write the meaning of each word. (Note: you're going to find some unusual words here, because we're going to use only bases that are words.) Use a dictionary if you need to. Note how the affix joins onto the word.

ad	adjoin	administer
com	commingle	compromise
in	incapable	insufficient
ob	oblong	obnoxious
sub	submarine	subsoil
syn	synoptic	synchronic

(Answers are on page 251.)

Ad it up

There are TEN allomorphs for *ad* (including *ad* itself). The prefix *ad* turns to *a-* before *sc, sp, st,* and *gn.* Otherwise, *ad*'s consonant matches the consonant it precedes either by doubling it or making a sound easy to pronounce.

Allomorph	Sample Word
ac	accompany acquaintance
ad	adjoin
af	affirm
ag	aggrieve
al	allot
an	annotate
ap	appetite
ar	arrest
as	assort
at	attune

How do you know if the word part you're looking at is an allomorph of *ad-* or some other morpheme? Look at the etymology in the dictionary entry. For example, if you look up *accompany* and look at the etymology all the way back to the origins of the word, it will say something like *ad + compaignon.* That *ad* in the etymology tells you that *ac* is an allomorph of *ad.*

Did you notice how many doubled consonants there are at the syllable juncture of the prefix and the root or base word, like in *accompany?* That's one of the signs of an assimilated prefix.

BRAIN TICKLERS
Set # 92

Find one example of a word for each allo-morph of *ad*. It can be attached to a base word or a root word.

(Answers are on page 252.)

In at the beginning

There are five allomorphs of *in-*.

Allomorph of *in*	Sample Word
i (before *g*)	ignominy
il (before *l*)	illegal
im (before *b, m, p*)	immortal
in (the rest of the time)	incapable
ir (before *r*)	irrational

BRAIN TICKLERS
Set # 93

Find two examples of words for each allomorph of *in*. They can be attached to a base word or a root word. How many of the ten have a doubled consonant at the syllable juncture between the prefix and the root or base word?

(Answers are on page 252.)

Don't let *com* con you

	Sample Word
Before *b*, *m*, and *p*, it's *com*.	combine
	complain
	commerce
Before *h*, *g*, *gn*, and usually before vowels, it's *co*.	cogent
	coherent
	cognition
Before *l*, it's *col* and before *r*, it's *cor*.	collaborate
	corroborate
Before other consonants, it's *con*.	conjecture

BRAIN TICKLERS
Set # 94

Find a word for each allomorph of *com* and use them to write a poem.

(Answers are on page 252.)

Toward an understanding of *ob*

o before *m*	omit
oc before *c*	occur
of before *f*	offend
op before *p*	oppose
ob the rest of the time	observe

Sub-pose we learn about *sub*

Sub is not just for submarines! Take a look.

suc before *c*	succeed
suf before *f*	suffix
sug before *g*	suggest
sum before *m*	summon
sup before *p*	suppose
sur before *r*	surreptitious
sus sometimes before *c, p, t*	suspect
sub before all else	submarine

BRAIN TICKLERS
Set # 95

Find a *sub* or *ob* word to match each clue. A hint tells you which allomorph to use for each.

1. Under the basement (*sub*)
2. No longer in use (*ob*)
3. Brief and clear (*suc*)
4. To enslave (*op*)
5. To maintain (*sus*)
6. To make something available (*sup*)

(Answers are on page 252.)

Syn is with us

Last one. Are you ready?

sym before *b, m, p*	symbiotic, symmetrical, sympathy
syl before *l*	syllable
sy before *s* and *z*	system, syzygy
syn elsewhere	syntax

BRAIN TICKLERS
Set # 96

Match the words with the definitions.

Words	Clues
1. syllogism	a. set of signs that indicates a disease
2. symphony	b. combining of different belief systems
3. synchronize	c. to happen in unison
4. syncretism	d. long sonata for orchestra
5. syndrome	e. point at which a celestial body is in conjunction with the sun
6. syzygy	f. reasoning from the general to the specific

And on that excellent spelling bee word—syzygy—we end.

(Answers are on page 252.)

BRAIN TICKLERS—
THE ANSWERS

Set # 89, page 240

D → S
extension
DE → S

collision	explosion	persuasion
decision	inclusion	
delusion	invasion	

CE → C

production	reduction

C → CI

mathematician	politician
musician	statistician

Set # 90, page 242

re**ceive** + tion	*e*	reception
per**ceive** + tion	*e*	preception
de**ceive** +tion	*e*	deception
state + ic	drop *e*	static
tone + ic	drop *e*	tonic
bile + ious	drop *e*	bilious
grain + ular	drop *i*	granular
mime + ic	drop *e*	mimic
flame +able	drop *e*	flammable

Set # 91, page 244

adjoin	to be next to
administer	to direct
commingle	to mingle with
compromise	to settle differences with
incapable	not capable
insufficient	not sufficient
oblong	elongated in one direction
obnoxious	very annoying
submarine	a ship that can operate beneath the water
subsoil	the layer of earth under the topsoil
synoptic	presenting a report from the same point of view
synchronic	occurring at the same time

Set # 92, page 246

Possible responses:

a	ascend	**ag**	aggravate	**ar**	arrange
ac	accustom, acquire	**al**	allocate	**as**	assimilate
ad	admire	**an**	announce	**at**	attend
af	affix	**ap**	appall		

Set # 93, page 247

Possible responses:

i	ignore, ignoble	**in**	inaccurate, inappropriate
il	illegible, illuminate	**ir**	irresponsible, irregular
im	immaterial, immature		Six have a doubled consonant.

Set # 94, page 248

Possible responses:

co	coexist	**com**	compare
col	collect	**con**	construct conclude (one extra!)
cor	correct		

How can I <u>construct</u> a poem that makes sense
When I'm feeling rather dense?
How many allomorphs must I <u>collect</u>?
It's hard to get them all <u>correct</u>.
Why should so many forms <u>coexist</u>?
I have to keep adding to my list.
When each prefix I <u>compare,</u>
I just <u>conclude</u> it isn't fair.

Set # 95, page 249

1. subbasement
2. obsolete
3. succinct
4. oppress
5. sustain
6. supply

Set # 96, page 250

1. f
2. d
3. c
4. b
5. a
6. e

INDEX

*Pages in boldface indicate where terms are defined.

INDEX